PRAISE FOR THE
GROWTH RESOURCES INDICATOR (GRI)

"We've used the GRI for a number of things. Recruiting is a big area, but also we've used it to understand our staff and our management team, and also to understand the relationships between people and how we interact with each other. I think it's absolutely vital to attend the seminar. As a result, it's made me much more effective in quickly using the GRI for different purposes in my company. "
   — George Northup, CEO of Author-IT

"We have found that the GRI gives our team the opportunity to discuss what each employee brings and what we want to bring into the team culture with each new hire. We have no time to waste. Anything that helps us get to a better state more efficiently and effectively is important to us. That's why we like the GRI."
   — Mary Lou Song, executive chairman of FuelX

"GRI has really improved our confidence in our hiring process. We give it to everybody and it really helps us to pinpoint a word to probe and it really helps, especially when I'm looking for specific people, to see what to look for in the GRI profile."
   — Bob Fung, president of Owens Design

"Going and making the decision to be certified in the GRI was one of the greatest things that I have done so far. It's really impacted our company. The seminar in itself was very intense, but I knew that it was going to make a huge impact on the decisions that I made for the future of our company, for the teams that we put together."

— Krystle Warren, business operations manager at Structure Law Group

"We use the GRI as an invaluable system in recruiting and aligning our teams of data scientists and engineers. Two Six Capital is a technology company that has pioneered data science for private equity. Our team is amphibious, combining the best of Silicon Valley tech and Wall Street-styled deal culture. The GRI's data-driven, benchmarked approach gives us the right insights to continually develop our unique firm culture."

— Sajjad Jaffer, managing partner of Two Six Capital

"My team and I have worked with the GRI over the years for our talent recruitment. We find this system not only relevant to our activity, but also accurate, saving us much time and energy to eradicate hiring mistakes. Moreover, GRI is a medium that develops a trusted relationship between our people faster and stronger. It's especially important to us as our company operates globally, encompassing several cultures and nationalities. In fact, we believe GRI is an amazing solution for any executive interested in improving her people skills and leadership."

— François Dubrulle, CEO of The Green Airliner

"One of the really powerful elements of the GRI platform is to allow the management team or a group of individual contributors to get visibility into their peers and to understand how their peers may interact in a very different function, from engineering to sales, and therefore how better to work with each other. This has helped dramatically from a team-dynamics perspective and to allow me to build the culture of the organization."

— Adrian Hall, CEO of CF Engine

"When you're meshing people together, the result is actually a very beautiful thing and you actually end up recognizing the unique ability of everyone, knowing that you cannot do this alone, that you actually need to have someone very different than you, to deliver the highest level of service. And the GRI has helped us do that."

— Helen Dietz, director of wealth management at Aspiriant and former president and CEO of Stanford Investment Group

"If you're looking at leadership as getting the right people in the right job, then a big component that GRI brings to you is a more effective understanding of the dynamic of teams, and helping teams to identify the balance that they need for each role. GRI is about engineering how everybody can show up and do what they're best at, and aren't forced to work against their strengths because that's what is required of the job."

— S. Rose Vaughan, corporate director of people and culture at Bacchus Restaurant Management Group

"There are many individual assessments out there—DISC, Kolbe, PI, Gallup—and they're all useful up to a point. But only GRI deals with the real world: individuals in relationships, teams, and organizations. Until you have looked at your people in context and modeled possible changes to teams, you don't know the real value of what you're missing. I couldn't imagine going back to the old way."

– Marcus Clarke-Goss, principal at REDW

"The GRI has been a fantastic part of our business. Hiring is really a necessity, and it's something that we try to delegate as much as possible. One of the things GRI has done is to really save a lot of time and zero in on the prospects we feel would be the best fit from the very beginning. Now I don't have to spend hundreds of hours quite literally reviewing resumes from applicants for various positions like I used to. So it's been really helpful for us in our organization, helpful from me as an executive. And I would strongly encourage anyone who's looking to speed up the process to get a deeper insight into what makes our employees tick or make the recruitment process easier and I would certainly recommend the GRI."

– Scott Kirk, CEO of Interluxe

LEAD
BEYOND
INTUITION

How to Build a
High-Performing Organization

Frederic Lucas-Conwell, PhD

To my wife
and better half, Susan

CONTENTS

PART II. THE POWER OF A VISUAL LANGUAGE

PART III. THE PATH TO MASTERING PERFORMANCE

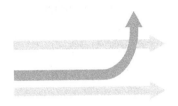

THE CHALLENGE ALL CEOS FACE

The real voyage of discovery consists not in
seeking new landscapes, but in having new eyes.
— **Marcel Proust**

The biggest challenge that any leader seeking to run a successful organization faces is finding and retaining the right people for their company. Insightful leadership doesn't have value until team members perform in their jobs. The challenge is evidenced by a growing disconnect within organizations. For instance, 51 percent of employees are not engaged and 16 percent are actively disengaged at work[1]; 70 percent of mergers *reduce* shareholder worth or, at best, have a neutral impact on it—this poor performance is most often caused by employees and company culture.[2]

After all, a company is only as good as its people. Yet, what I have learned from my experience as an entrepreneur and as a researcher

---

1   Gallup, "Gallup 2016 Q[12] Meta-Analysis Report," 2016.
2   KPMG, "Why Most Acquisitions Fail," January 2017.

of human behavior in the workplace is that the information available to organizations for recruiting, evaluating, and making decisions about team members is often subjective and incomplete.

Finding the right employees to propel your organization forward can take months, if not years, and oftentimes hiring top talent is not enough if they languish in the wrong role or team. Discovering how we and others can perform at our best requires patience and introspection. Paradoxically, our intuition about people is the most ancient and primal kind of knowledge that lives within us. But taking that gut-level knowledge to the next level has proven to require time and experience to develop.

What if there was a way to accelerate and expand this process? Even better, a method for removing intuition's biases when identifying and aligning talent within your organization? A strategy for framing an individual's capacity to grow and perform with regard to the expectations of others, like the requirements of a specific job and the needs of other teammates? Could we perhaps reduce the time and money wasted on bad personnel decisions by developing a quality assessment of how people and their organizations perform?

As an entrepreneur who started my first company at age twenty-six and grew the number of employees from one to thirty-five in four years, this put a lot of pressure on me to quickly improve my management skills. I had a hard time finding sound advice about managing the "people parts" of my business.

Rapidly, employee aspects began taking up most of my time (my rough estimate is 85 percent). Interviewing was time consuming, recruiting—especially of salespeople—was frustrating, and employee turnover was costly. Although I found reading business books by

Peter Drucker, Garry Hamel, and other authors to be thought provoking, these books did not include any practical advice for the day-to-day hiring and managing of people.

In the mid-1990s, I decided to take advantage of the growing science about the human personality, having already experienced most major assessments, and use these tools myself, as the CEO, for recruiting. This was quite uncommon since only HR specialists or clinical psychologists usually accessed these techniques. However, graphology, astrology, and other "ology" techniques were in vogue among executives in Europe, and, as I discovered later, pretty much everywhere else—if not directly, through consultants. I decided to dive more deeply into what these tools could reveal and how they could be used to empower employees and optimize organizations.

At that time, the public was becoming more familiar with techniques such as the Myers-Briggs Type Indicator® (MBTI). In the recruiting world, different personality techniques had been popular for a while, including the 16PF® from Raymond Cattell, a British-American pioneer in personality research. Service companies and consultants—not yet called executive coaches—were beginning to take advantage of these techniques.

Looking back at what these techniques were thirty years ago is like watching the early age of aviation. The first planes flew short distances and crashed often. They were progressively replaced with newer models that did not require any skills in mechanics and were soon flying across the ocean.

Older assessment techniques may still be in use today, but with time, their limitations have become clear, and many of them are now history. Assessment techniques have evolved for use in education and the workplace, using larger data sets and new statistics on people in these environments, and allowing greater refinement in what needs to be measured and how.

My first enterprise continued to grow, eventually received venture capital financing, and acquired a larger company along the way. The computer-aided design and manufacturing market that we were competing in was evolving quickly, and we were fortunate to successfully restructure and sell the company to a competitor at the right time. This created a unique opportunity to refocus my energy on my new passion: understanding personality and how to utilize it to maximize performance in the workplace. This was not what my education in engineering had prepared me to do, but my recent business experience inspired me to delve more deeply into those areas.

When we set out to create Growth Resources Indicators (GRI), our aim was to take advantage of the most recent findings in the science of personality and organizational behavior, reveal more effectively the talents and motivations of individual team members, help utilize this information at both team and organization levels, and enlighten CEOs and other executives about what's really going on inside their organizations so that they can reach new levels of performance.

As our research progressed it became clear that the metrics we make use of in production, sales, finance, and other Key Performance Indicators (KPI) are insufficient for managing a company's performance. How people act, emotionally adapt, develop a sense of purpose, and get engaged at work all play a large role in the success of individuals, teams, and ultimately the entire organization. Measuring and managing these elements need to be part of an organization's core metrics and mastered by its executives.

The inescapable fact is that, as human beings, we are all limited in our comprehension of what makes us and others tick. But by designing objective measurements and a common language around how to better decipher people and their behavior, we can help motivate them and grow their talents.

Moreover, we have learned that when team members acknowledge the core of their personality and how it affects their behavior, they can not only improve their individual performance, but also the performance of their organizations, dramatically.

We've had the opportunity to work with companies that are under intense pressure to grow and be a part of an ecosystem made of investors, lawyers, executives, consultants, and many others striving for success. In the process, we have gathered, synthetized, and refined a vast amount of information from the social science and management fields. We've combined more than twenty years' worth of experiences and observations with on-the-ground research, interviewing nearly 1,100 people in 500 companies across five continents.

Although the lessons contained in this book originated from our research on the use of personality assessment in organizations, those lessons are also informed by feedback from thousands of people and hundreds of companies. From Palo Alto and Singapore to Paris and worldwide, the experiences of leaders and managers who have implemented the GRI into their organizations have been incorporated into our findings. Whatever their diverse origins, all organizations share an interest in finding more effective ways for recognizing how we can perform, recruit, and manage people better.

As a result, we've established a philosophy of cultivating talent that is personal, nuanced, and offers everyone and their organizations the prospect of succeeding on their own terms.

WHAT'S AHEAD

In Part I, we confront the personnel challenges that all organizations must grapple with and demonstrate how breakthroughs in the collection and analysis of individualized data offers new solutions to these problems. Part I demonstrates the fundamental need for tools to assess what's happening throughout your organization and what's needed for its future, and how learning at a higher speed is necessary for acquiring the skills to take your leadership to the next level.

We describe how to reach a nuanced understanding of what motivates people, intrinsically and extrinsically, in the workplace. We reveal how personality assessments can help us steer clear of our implicit biases.

Part II explains the GRI behavior profile, its components, and what exactly personality assessments should measure when attempting to analyze people's performance at work.

Making sense of individual behavior then leads to deeper insights into how organizations of people interact, work together, and succeed. If you have already read other books or papers on the GRI, this material may look familiar.

In Part III, we examine how what we saw in the first and second parts can be put into practice. Learning about and applying assessment tools enables organizations to more accurately define the natural strengths needed when recruiting for a specific role or when staffing a team.

For example, when the behavior profiles are used to assess job demands, interactions between team members, and the overall needs of the organization, they give leaders insight on how best to design and staff an organization's teams and strategize its growth so that all teammates can work efficiently and feel fulfilled and purpose-driven in their position.

ONE MORE THING...

The examples included in this book are from real people and companies. In some cases, we have changed the names or details of circumstances to protect the identities of individuals and their organizations.

The people whose work has influenced this book are numerous. Referencing all of them in notes would have been impractical. Instead, we have listed the most influential books and articles in the bibliography.

Throughout the book we use an illustrated character to explain certain kinds of behavior. We tried to make the character as neutral as possible in order to avoid favoring any gender; though, we did design the character to look somewhat like a human being.

Trusting a new way of looking at ourselves and others and challenging our intuition about human behavior is difficult. This shift requires new lenses, and plenty of practice, to better see and comprehend people and the organizations they work in.

The learning process can be accelerated by transferring and sharing the knowledge that other users, experts, and researchers have already accumulated through those lenses. And that practice will generate the confidence to use such new knowledge quickly and effectively.

TAKING THE GRI SURVEY

Having your GRI behavior profile in hand will help you with the reading of this book. If you are a member of an organization that is covered by an annual Service and License Agreement (SLA) for the GRI, taking the GRI survey may come to you as part of this program.

Or you may go online to our website: **www.gri.co/lead**, create an account for accessing additional resources and take the survey. You can save 30% on the survey when you take it within 30 days of purchasing this book.

Once the survey is completed, you will receive your GRI behavior profile and options such as our Discovery program to review your results and their benefits by participating in webinars, sharing your results, or asking an advanced GRI user questions.

PART I

THE
TROUBLE
WITH
MANAGING
PEOPLE

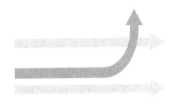

Chapter 1

THERE IS NO SECRET FORMULA

Every company's leadership, employees, and stakeholders dream of creating a product or service so successful that the demand for it outstrips their organization's ability to keep up with supply. And yet, organizations must be able to scale quickly if they want to fully capitalize on the momentum they've generated; otherwise they risk missing a prime opportunity for growth.

Expansion is one of the biggest challenges successful organizations face. Scaling a business and adding staff can easily trip up a young company. Luke Brawn, CEO of an industrial construction firm in the United States, knew this intimately from his experience growing his business from zero to $60 million over the past three decades.

Two years ago, Luke's executive team designed a strategic plan to grow the business and set goals to expand to $140 million a year over five years. In doing that, the company entered a period of tremendous growth and recognized the need for talented people at every level of the business: accounting, operations estimating, purchasing, drafting, field support, and safety inspection.

"I was looking for that secret formula, the secret pill that helps me eliminate bad hires," Luke explained. "We started interviewing for positions and we would hear people during the interview say words or phrases or things that they are capable of doing, only to find out that they weren't really capable of doing it more than they like doing it, but they knew they'd get a job if they answered it the right way."

One thing became crystal clear to Luke: the traditional method of hiring talent based on a person's resume qualifications, college pedigree, and in-person demeanor in a one-hour interview is broken. "I realized the amount of money I was spending on bad hires because they interviewed really well," he said.

In another case, Mark, the CEO of a direct mail marketing company in Europe, recalls a situation where a new hire tipped the balance of a team in the wrong direction. "There were these two guys who had been working perfectly well together, performing well above average, and a third joins the team. In a couple of hours, the two who had been good friends for years started to hate each other. The results went down the rabbit hole. The situation turned into a crisis. Some people are really talented at wreaking havoc, and they are a real threat for companies. The more you wait to solve these situations, the more they pervade the whole company, creating even more damage."

This problem is not unique to Luke's and Mark's organizations. Identifying, hiring, and retaining talent, along with many other challenges related to people management, are problems that all organizations must grapple with periodically, if not daily.

Why is it so difficult to efficiently manage people? One reason is that talent is an abstract concept that is difficult to quantify and qualify.

Moreover, different kinds of organizations and jobs call for different kinds of talents.

To complicate matters further, as humans we are wired to rely on our intuition about people, but our gut feelings are often proven wrong and can be influenced by unconscious biases. We indicate the most common ones below.

- *Stereotyping:* making preconceived opinions about a group of individuals

- *Selective perception:* a natural inclination towards our own needs, expectations, and values

- *Halo effect:* forming a general impression of a person or situation based on just one characteristic

- *Self-fulfilling prophecy:* the propensity to cause something to become true simply because we expect it to be true

The alternative is painstakingly building this knowledge about employees, candidates, and other stakeholders through trial and error, gaining insights through decades of experience.

But what if there was a better, more accurate, and objective way to measure talent and performance in the workplace?

THE ADVENT OF NEW TOOLS

The invention of new measuring tools allows us to better comprehend and communicate about the thing we are measuring. This was the case with telescopes in the early seventeenth century when it came to exploring the sky and theorizing about the location of Earth in the grand picture of the universe, starting with the Scientific Revolution and the Enlightenment. Ever since, telescopes have continued to challenge our imagination about the true nature of outer space and the cosmos, including the amazing color pictures recently rendered by the Hubble Space Telescope.

In a similar fashion, the Internet has given anyone with an Internet connection an avenue for enlarging their understanding of the world beyond their own backyard at the click of a button. When I travelled in remote parts of Asia in the late 1980s, I was the first foreigner many people there had ever seen. That's much less likely to happen in the post-Internet era where you can explore other peoples and parts of the world through YouTube videos and WhatsApp chats.

In both cases, the invention of the telescope and the Internet changed our perception of who we are by giving us a broader, more accurate perspective of the world we inhabit.

The history of personality assessments is short compared to the history of telescopes, although it begins earlier than the Internet. The first assessments emerged at the end of the 1890s and progressed slowly for decades; their evolution kicked into overdrive in the 1980s with the advent of personal computers.

As the philosophy and structure of personality assessments progressed, so too did technology and new methods of capturing people's individual data at a global scale with the help of the Internet, applied statistics, and techniques for comparing and aggregating data.

We developed Growth Resources Indicators (GRI) to measure aspects of individual behavior and performance in the workplace. The advent of new tools for collecting, mining, and understanding data on personality and behavior now offers us a more holistic and thorough way to look at organizations, as well as people. Today we can more easily compare jobs within and between organizations and contrast organizations of different sizes, cultures, industries, and countries. We can look at ourselves and better appreciate how we might perform in our job, team, and organization.

As a result, we've gotten smarter about people. The GRI's visual language and objective evaluation of human behavior, as it is expressed in the GRI behavior profiles, allows us to recognize what drives people, what motivates them, and how we can provide support in this process as managers. This leads to reduced friction, increased collaboration, greater organizational harmony, and higher productivity—which many of the companies we work with have already experienced.

WORK IN PROGRESS

Take, for example, Structure Law Group, a firm that specializes in business law in Silicon Valley. Using the GRI, founder Mark Figueiredo explained, allows their firm to "analyze how to pair team members up with other people, how to put them in positions where they can succeed. We've done that and now months, years later, when people start working and they encounter little issues, we refer back to the GRI and see how it was able to predict what they've actually experienced."

When organizations acknowledge who each of their team members are—how they prefer to work, what kind of motivation and feedback they respond to—they are not only able to harness the unique talents of their team, but they also build a culture where everyone is nurtured and set up to succeed. Team members stay with organizations when they feel valued.

Gokalp Gurer, a junior associate at Structure Law Group, first took the GRI survey when he was being recruited to work at the firm. Gokalp had never been asked to take a personality assessment for a job before, so he was initially skeptical. He was surprised to see how accurate the assessment was when he reviewed the results with his future supervisor. "When I was told that I prefer fast-paced, high-pressure work as opposed to routine work—of course, I felt like I could have told myself that, but the true value of the GRI was how these minute details were implemented in the office setting," Gokalp said.

Once he was hired, his GRI profile helped inform the way his supervisors managed him. "My supervisors avoid giving me routine work. They instill constant change in my assignments. For example, I am often rotating between incorporating companies and drafting motions and reviewing contracts, or going through discovery, or reviewing documents, all different types of assignments that are all at a different pace, that require different sets of skills, and require an attorney to tap into different parts of their brain and understanding. This constant, ever-changing, fast-paced environment is what really helps me to thrive. What I'm getting at is that without the GRI, it might have taken much longer to figure that out, not because I don't know myself and not because my manager might not have been able to tell, but learning that right off the bat when they hired me made for a much quicker transition period, and it allowed them to forecast ahead and pair me with other attorneys."

In other cases, the GRI profile can be instrumental in changing the way managers deal with interpersonal conflicts and how they communicate with team members, both individually and as a group. Sushila Sahay, an executive at Lightbend, a technology company headquartered in San Francisco, explained: "The GRI gives you a common language so you can talk about each other's characteristics and really understand what that means. It's so easy to make assumptions or use different words to say the same thing. You may actually be saying the same thing, but you don't realize it because you're interpreting words differently. The GRI profile gives you a common framework."

Lightbend's CEO, Mark Brewer, agreed: "The opportunity to use a system with a well-defined set of terms that define a person's personality makes it easier to have a conversation about situations that might be otherwise difficult. If you have somebody who is just stubborn or really hard to get your point across to, they won't move off the opinion they have. But when you look at their GRI profile, you not only know what's possibly causing that difficult conversation, but you also have a way to communicate with them in a less threatening way using the terms that come from the GRI."

In the following chapters, we discuss the universal challenges of managing a workforce and how new technologies and more reliable data on behavior can aid in tackling these issues.

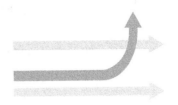

Chapter 2

HOW WE EVALUATE PEOPLE

For anyone in a management role, determining the right characteristics to assess—and learning how to evaluate people based on these characteristics—takes time.

Over time, most of us refine this process and its outcomes. We obtain new insights, plus more self-awareness and discipline, so that we can refrain from judging too fast. We begin to rely more on the characteristics and techniques that prove to be more useful. We challenge our gut feelings and intuition to stay a bit more distant, hopefully taking advantage of more objective and effective assessments.

I experienced that process myself when I started managing people. "Competence" and "interest" were the most basic characteristics to screen for before planning a first interview with candidates. "Intelligence" and "culture fit" were the most important to assess during interviews for predicting success in the job and within our company. But neither these characteristics nor the ways of assessing them were effective enough to better motivate our employees and improve our company's performance faster. I had my own personal technique too, which I called "looking people in the eyes," and I was already experiencing its limitations.

Researching personality assessments and how they can improve our performance and that of our organizations led me to analyze how such assessments generate their results. I became interested in how assessments are used by all potential users at organizations—not merely HR professionals, but CEOs, C-level executives, and individual contributors. How did these new measurements influence their thinking?

THE TECHNIQUES USED IN ASSESSMENT

Many different kinds of techniques can be used to assess a person's relevant characteristics; some are scientifically researched, while others are simply intuitive strategies that can be hard to express or replicate. An individual's characteristics typically span a wide range of possibilities, including how competent or smart the person is, their education, diploma, some physical attributes, and many other characteristics that we may not even be able to verbalize, which constitute our intuition about people.

Although the following example may surprise you, it's one of the many stories captured during our fieldwork that illustrates how knowledge about people builds and gets anchored to a characteristic and the assessment process.

The founder of a rental car company assessed job candidates through what I refer to as the "walking up the stairs" technique. He would welcome candidates at the reception desk and always follow them to his office on the second floor, walking up the stairs to get there. Some climbed the stairs silently and fast; others took their time and chitchatted. Some candidates had clean shoes and were properly dressed, others not so much. According to the founder, his twenty-second "walking up the stairs" assessment was the most informative part of his meetings with candidates and the biggest influence on his final decision to recruit them. Most of his recruits turned out to become valuable employees of the company, although there were a few exceptions.

Typical employee assessments are simply how we think about candidates. The characteristics we use to judge them come with knowledge and experience—propositions that may prove to be true and useful for recruitment, communication, management, and making other important decisions or recommendations.

When we conduct an assessment, we may call for assistance from search consultants, coaches, other advisers, or even artificial intelligence. Or we can call for a collective decision by involving others in our organization. But in either case, assisted or not, it goes back to the fact that we each have our set of anchored characteristics in mind, all of which strongly influence the way we recruit and manage people.

THE PATCHWORK OF TALENTS

To display all the prevalent characteristics we make use of in our assessment, and show where those traits stand, we came up with the idea of the talent patchwork. Everyone possesses a unique mix of skills, intelligence, knowledge, values, and experience—a colorful patchwork of characteristics that make up who they are.

The behavioral/emotional aspects of our personality that can be assessed through interviews and personality assessments—how we behave, how we engage emotionally, and why we are motivated to perform—are represented in the middle of the patchwork.

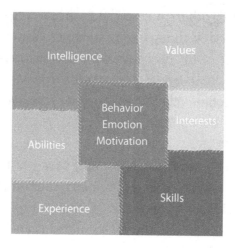

Working with the GRI over the years has helped to define the patchwork's components and use them more efficiently, bringing clarity to the different psychological characteristics and providing critical information for their development.

When viewed together as part of an individual's talent patchwork, these characteristics represent a fuller, more complete picture of an individual's potential. Talent, like competency or value, is a broad concept that has evolved into the belief that everyone possesses characteristics that can be viewed as positive. They simply need to be discovered and developed.

There are new constraints put on the way we evaluate people's performance when those individuals become part of an organization, take on job responsibilities, and are compensated for their work. New challenges and criteria emerge in a professional context and the context of how people behave in a family setting or at school recedes. This changes the focus of the characteristics that people need to possess; being competent and skilled takes on a whole new meaning.

ONLY ASSESS THE CHARACTERISTICS THAT MATTER

Jane and Bob, who work at the same firm, are more than a collection of characteristics or concepts. They are human beings with a history, a sense of purpose, needs and motivations to satisfy, and much more.

Characteristics are numerous, but some are less malleable, harder to learn, and more important than others for discerning our talent and how we perform in a job.

In the software industry, the ratio of developers with exceptional skills to developers with lower skills is known to be as high as one to fifty. This has made assessing a developer's speed at coding and building clear, effective algorithms and architecting a software product a critical step. Experience and knowledge come second after a developer's innate cognitive skills and potential to continue developing their knowledge base at high speed.

The talent patchwork offers a framework for determining the important characteristics that need to be better understood and evaluated at recruitment time and beyond, encouraging a more objective integration of personality characteristics into your analysis of people.

Being clear about how candidates need to perform and what a personality assessment can potentially measure helps refine the understanding of those important personal characteristics and how they get expressed and grow over time. People's behavior is always present; it occurs in the midst of and alongside all the other characteristics in the talent patchwork.

The information and insights that are revealed by how people perform plays a critical role in developing new talent, including new competencies, interests, and skills—not only technical skills, but interpersonal skills—with accuracy and speed.

Once you see and comprehend an individual's preferences, you realize that a lack of intelligence, interest, or skill may not be the problem. Rather, it's the mismatch in role and personality. What becomes more challenging, though, is accurately assessing the other facets of the talent patchwork and providing support for their growth.

The information captured by the talent patchwork can be used at recruitment time for identifying talent and making sure you keep in mind important aspects of the job, as well as by employees, managers, and leaders to further advance their personal growth, self-awareness, team dynamics, and leadership development.

THE TWO-STEP PROCESS

There are two fundamental steps in the process of assessing people:

1. We build hypotheses about the characteristics we assess based on our own experience. The characteristics we choose to assess are influenced by how we listen, read, and interact with advisors, mentors, and other influencers; by the management books of our time; by the culture and values of our organization; by other characteristics that we are used to, are more intimate with, or have not even verbalized yet.

2. Then we experiment with our hypothesis about these characteristics by testing and working with them. If our assumption about them is proven to be true on a small sample of people and has practical relevance, we continue making use of these characteristics in a larger sample by including more and more people in the experimentation.

This two-step process allows us to outline how the characteristics continue being useful and true for assessing people, along with progressively building knowledge of their limitations. We re-actualize what the implications are for ourselves in managing individuals by what we think, say, do or not do with these characteristics and the knowledge we continue building on them. Or we decide to drop these characteristics after observing that they were too often false, restrictive, and ineffective. This leaves room for replacing our assumptions about characteristics and techniques with new ones we can test.

Some of these characteristics are only helpful when we make decisions on a day-to-day basis. Research suggests that we can assess a person on no more than five characteristics at any given time. We consequently have the tendency of using just a few of them that are usually the most effective for managing people.

There is nothing new here about how human beings build knowledge, draw inferences in a deductive or inductive manner, and attach meaning to symbolic features. The two-step process is solely an adaptation of how assessments work for us, based on how we build and draw inferences from their characteristics.

TECHNIQUES EVOLVE SLOWLY

More often than not, our ability and methods for assessing people evolve slowly. This is echoed by the work of Carol Dweck, a professor at Stanford University who developed mindset theory as a way to understand how we think about a person's behavior and assess their potential for growth. Some people are narrow and fixed in the characteristics they ascribe to people. At the other end of the spectrum, there are people who keep an open mind in their judgment of others and their ability to grow their talents.

The assessment techniques we use for assessing characteristics in the talent patchwork are part of who we are as humans. They are present and active in us before and after we interact with someone. They come with some expectations about the position that needs to be filled, even before someone is hired. The assessment process continues after recruitment according to how we pay attention to and nurture the individual now in the job and how we communicate and make decisions about him or her. It continues when we communicate about that person.

We make use of characteristics and techniques for assessing people until we feel limited by them. Mastering the contours of these limitations takes years, and navigating the "gray area" may leave us indecisive.

The learning and cleansing process happens through trial and error: recruiting workers who ultimately do not perform well in their job; not promoting others who could have been the perfect match; treating teammates in a way that is not as efficient as it could be if we spoke, paid attention, looked at them, made decisions or forgot to, etc.

The CEO of the rental car company had used and refined his "walking up the stairs" technique for more than four decades when he told me about it. The whole company made jokes about it. The test was part of the company's culture. Every employee had passed it. The process was indeed well refined and mastered by its architect: the CEO, until the company had to move to a place with no stairs, which came at a time when the technique began showing other weaknesses.

THE MANAGER'S PATCHWORK

All leaders and managers have their own talent patchworks. When considering people for specific roles, we refer to characteristics that we are comfortable with. Our comfort zone, not only for recruiting, but also for managing our relationships with people, is based on our individual talent patchwork.

Jane's belief that attending a specific school is a prerequisite for success is the key characteristic she relies on for recruiting and promoting employees. Although there have been regular demonstrations that attending a specific school does not guarantee success in a job, or that a variety of educational backgrounds benefits an organization, that will not deter Jane's belief unless she faces several negative experiences that challenge her assumption and force her to reconsider.

Bob's belief in people's intelligence as the ultimate predictor of success will endure until it reveals its limitations.

The point here is that whatever talent patchwork is decided upon for a specific position, one of the managers will not be aligned with it. This applies especially to psychological characteristics that are harder to pinpoint or describe. Whatever the organization may want to do to create alignment with these indefinable characteristics, it may go against the managers' beliefs about what makes a person talented and a good fit for the job.

REMOVING UNNECESSARY BIASES AND FRICTION

We can start removing major biases when we assess people by making use of more objective assessments and identifying the optimum characteristics needed in the talent patchwork with regard to the demands of a specific job. In return, this helps organizations better frame an individual's capacity to grow and perform in a job and provide adequate support for their success.

Still, trusting a new way of looking at ourselves and others by making use of more objective techniques and challenging our own assessment of human behavior is difficult.

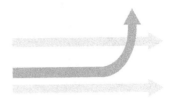

Chapter 3

A SCIENTIFIC WAY TO
MEASURE BEHAVIOR

A personality assessment has the potential to access the core of our personality—how we behave—rather than the outcome of our behavior itself.

What emerges from working with personality assessments is that the behaviors we find at our core are flexed and adapted at the cost of hard work that may ultimately be undesirable. How we adapt our behavior, the limits of its adaptation, and the emotional labor involved will be discussed below. With that in mind, whatever is at the core of our personality drives what we do and how we think, act, and perform in different situations.

Each individual has his or her own way of performing, taking different routes to the same destination. Accomplishing task #1 today and task #2 tomorrow requires us to adapt to different behaviors over time as illustrated below.

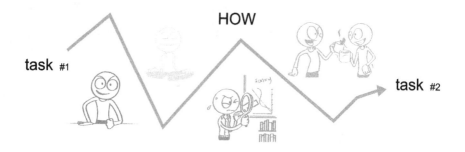

The outcome of a task or a specific set of actions can be easily identified based on observable, measurable facts.

> Outcomes belong to the world of Key Performance Indicators (KPIs) and data. But how we perform or bring about a specific outcome is the intangible element in the equation that is difficult to accurately observe and define.

How and why somebody completes a task depends on a convergence of forces, such as self-confidence, dexterity, compliance, social activities, the speed and intensity level at which we execute, and much more. It depends on our own individual and unique needs or drives to perform in general, as well as in specific situations, like an actor would on stage, acting out a role in a specific play.

DIMENSIONS OF PERSONALITY

Personality assessments were originally created by assuming that people have traits and that traits can be measured. Indeed, any trait—or what we could call a trait—can be measured and constructed with a personality assessment.

More and more evidence showed that the content of the traits being assessed could overlap greatly, and what was really being measured became more dubious. Two traits might use different labels but refer to the same content and, thus, become misleading.

Considering core dimensions revealed to be a more promising approach. Analyzing personality dimensions starts with the words we use to describe human behavior. Researchers call these words, which can be adjectives or nouns, descriptors or markers of personality. Personality markers are used to communicate about how we act, perform, or are expected to perform. Analyzing how these markers aggregate and overlap can eventually lead to more meaningful concepts.

We do not assume that these markers have an objective definition that we all agree on, but they do capture a kind of common sense about people's behavior and as such are useful. But we all have our own distinct understanding of these markers, which are ambiguous by nature.

The number of markers across languages is vast. In the English lexicon, there are nearly 18,000 words used for this purpose. There are 12,700 markers in French, 10,900 in German, and 11,000 in Italian.

Personality researchers have different methods for reducing the number of markers by stripping away those that are rarely used, obsolete, or inappropriate. At the end of this cleansing process, we're left with 400 to 700 words, depending on the language, that more commonly describe observed behaviors.

By applying a technique called factorial analysis, this pool of words is further reduced to a maximum of seven dimensions or factors that reflect personality and behavior. Because of the intense calculations required to select the appropriate markers, reduce their numbers, and condense them into seven factors or less, conduct research studies, and then analyze the results by running advanced statistics, it's only recently that we have been able to benefit from factorial analysis, first in the academic world for research, and more recently in the business world.

The number of dimensions has evolved over the years—from two to seven can be used depending on the study, how calculations were made, and the study's ultimate objective. It has become clear over time that these few dimensions form the building blocks of our personality, and that we can measure them by using the assessment technique.

Through our own research, we were able to identify replicable personality factors in different languages that can assist in understanding individuals across cultures, genders, and ages in work-related scenarios. This led us to define the four factors that became the core constituents of the GRI profile, which we will explain later.

A DEEPER DIVE INTO PERSONALITY

While the definition of "personality" can include intelligence, as well as other psychological characteristics, science has separated the concept into three different streams of focus. The first two groups of characteristics are most often referred to as the "cognitive" and "behavioral/emotional." A third group combines concepts that we find at the junction of the other two groups, such as competencies, skills, or interests. We sometimes refer to this third group of characteristics as the "conative."

These three groups have been around since the ancient times of the Greeks; more recent research has helped refine our interpretation of them. For now, we want to focus on the behavioral/emotional component of our personality, where many discoveries have been made in the past decades.

According to the research, personality dimensions have a relative stability and consistency over time. Many personality dimensions can be measured in the workplace, but a limited number of them focused on behavior apply to all individuals across cultures and countries. We eventually adapt and change. Although our personality dimensions may evolve, they are comparatively stable. Those two things—focusing on a limited number of dimensions and comparative stability over time—are important aspects that research has studied at length.

NATURAL AND PREDICTABLE BEHAVIORS AT WORK

A central premise in personality theories is that the behavior we exhibit, or at a minimum some aspects of it, is consistent over time. Should we retake a personality assessment at different intervals, the results should be similar.

Longitudinal studies conducted on personality assessments, especially those that were devised in academia for assessing traits, have long provided evidence of this consistency. However, this finding does not hold true for all assessments, especially since the dimensions being measured are so different and measured in so many different ways, including techniques that measure typologies rather than traits.

In addition, the consistency of a dimension over time varies from one individual to another; some individuals are more consistent than others. Few change radically, most may adapt moderately to the situations or circumstances they find themselves in, and few remain 100 percent consistent over a long period like ten years or more.

To answer the question, "Is Joe going to behave this way?" we first have to agree on what "behave this way" means. Some people display behaviors that are frequently observable, intense, and highly probable, while others do so less frequently and intensely. One way to answer this question is to consider how Joe's specific way of behaving can be assessed by a technique, consistently and reliably over time.

In addition, although there is evidence that we display certain behaviors more naturally and spontaneously—some systems refer to them as preferences—we adapt our behaviors to specific environments, including our work environment. These aspects of adaptation are critical and we discuss them fully below.

The other premise of using personality assessment in the context of an organization is that the dimensions being assessed must relate to work. Since assessments are created for different applications, and eventually used for purposes that are not related to working in organizations, this aspect is another important one to consider. Some personality dimensions may look interesting but may have nothing to do with work or at least in the normal range of behavior that we are interested in considering at work. The most extreme example of this is when dimensions are assessed for clinical diagnoses, such as depression, kleptomania, and bipolarity, which may solely be appropriate for doctors, but not for non-clinicians who want to better evaluate people in organizations.

As evidenced during our fieldwork, systems that assess personality are far from being constant with regard to the two previously stated premises. How predictable a behavior is cannot be conceded for sure, especially when what is being measured is a typology, such as being an introvert or extrovert—people may easily change types. That the personality dimensions measured by an assessment are related to work cannot be assumed either; looking at the assumptions under which the dimensions were built can serve as a check.

WHAT DRIVES BEHAVIOR

Our emotions are integral to us and how we behave, and they need to be taken into account when assessing our unique personalities. Three other concepts are important in regard to personal and organizational development:

- **Motivation**: We are affected and motivated internally by what's happening within us, which is a product of who we are and our experiences. Our motivation is affected by our environment, which includes other people. Engagement is created by each individual's unique motivation.

- **Goals**: Setting and pursuing goals comes naturally as a result of how we act and how we feel a need to adapt. We self-regulate our goals based on how we perceive the need to do so.

- **Learning**: Constant growth stimulates, engages, and helps us to retain, refine, and enjoy the experience of learning new skills. Just as we are motivated and set goals in different ways, we each learn and are encouraged to learn in different ways, too.

An important aspect that needs to be assessed is the unique way that each of us perceives and reacts to our environment, both emotionally and intellectually. Also unique is the way we adapt to the workplace in order to perform in our designated roles, as we perceive the need for it. Each of us finds certain experiences engaging, stimulating, motivating, and fulfilling, while other experiences can make us feel sad, discouraged, unmotivated, and unhappy.

How we act and react to our environment is closely related to the positive and negative emotions that we experience while doing so, especially when we are adjusting our most natural behavior.

Adapting to our environment, away from our natural way of per-forming, can be demanding and involve emotional labor. The strain of adapting to fit expectations, when the distance between what is natural to us and what is expected is too great, can take a toll on us. Too much adaptation may put serious limitations on our ability to sustain motivation and achieve expected goals.

What if we could anticipate the effort required to adapt to any given role and prevent or contain the negative consequences of stretch-ing ourselves or someone else too far? These aspects of adaptation are critical for any workplace where individual performance and effectiveness are of primary importance. We will discuss those aspects in the next chapter.

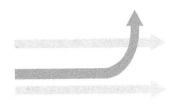

Chapter 4

WHY WE WORK

Professional actors can, impressively, transform into different characters from one movie to another. For instance, Meryl Streep in the movie *Florence Foster Jenkins* is undoubtedly a different person from the woman she plays in *The Devil Wears Prada*. In the first film, she plays Florence Foster Jenkins, a meek, flighty American socialite who was publicly mocked for her terrible singing. In the second film, Streep plays Miranda Priestly, a diabolical, powerful, bossy editor-in-chief at a high fashion magazine. The two characters could not be further apart. It's incredible to see the same actor embody and bring to life significantly different roles from movie to movie. Meryl Streep is Meryl Streep, not Florence or Miranda, and she is motivated to engage in two distinct, contrasting movie roles.

Onstage and offstage are two different realities for actors. There is the character they play in a specific movie, that part of them we see on screen. And there is the person they are when they are at home with their family and friends with whom they share their real or natural self.

> The amount of effort it takes actors to perform a role that is distant from their natural identity can lead to psychological adjustments that require a great deal of preparation and recovery. Acting out roles that are close to their natural character not only feels more consistent, but also generates less emotional stress.

In the same way that actors act and adapt to a role, the rest of us do the same in the workplace and attempt to match the demands of our position. In companies, it is the position that connects us to our organization, to coworkers, and to managers and their expectations. The behaviors required by these positions also need to be understood.

How we perceive the requirements of our position is important to consider from a behavioral standpoint. Our perception informs the motivation we derive from our job, whether we are engaged or not, and the type of support we may need in order to successfully adapt.

WHERE MOTIVATION COMES FROM

With his publication of the book *A Theory of Human Motivation* in the 1940s, Abraham Maslow may have been the first person to bring forward a theory that revolutionized the way we think about motivation. He established a clear hierarchy of needs: physical needs come first; we need to breathe, eat, and sleep. Then come safety, social needs, esteem such as prestige and power, and finally the need for self-actualization, such as developing greater competencies, achieving goals, or earning more money.

Other motivational theories followed Maslow's, including the two-factor theory from Frederick Herzberg, in which satisfaction and dissatisfaction need to be regarded in parallel, rather than as the two extremities of the same continuum. As it turns out with the two-factor theory, reducing dissatisfaction does not lead to greater motivation, but to a momentary pause in being dissatisfied and demotivated.

Having a motivated and engaged workforce in our organizations requires tapping into other needs, such as those described by Maslow. For instance, providing perks, raising salary, or social benefit rewards momentarily reduce both dissatisfaction and demotivation in the workplace, but may not increase motivation.

With Edgar Vroom came the expectancy theory, the first theory to recognize that individuals are cognizant of and motivated to select specific behaviors over others based on the results they expect from those behaviors. A person's effort on a task depends on the perception they have of what will happen when they achieve the desired outcome.

The above theoretical frameworks, while offering a basis for understanding motivation and providing broad answers from different angles, are not sufficiently specific about motivation on an individual level.

DIFFERENT PEOPLE, DIFFERENT MOTIVATIONS

We are all sensitive to different motivators and need to be rewarded in different ways.

As it has been repeatedly shown, money is not the almighty motivator and reward that some suppose it to be. Surveys done as far back as the 1940s show that good working conditions, an appreciation of the work done, management support for employees, and job security can indeed be better motivators than money itself. How much so depends on the industry, how rewards are dispensed in a unique location, and the specific country where the work is done.

> **Motivation in Brief**
> Our motivation can be considered in different ways, including through a hierarchy of needs based on what is desirable and not, by satisfying some expectations or receiving attention. Intrinsic and extrinsic motivations depend on how we act and perceive the need to adapt to the environment.

The Hawthorne experiment in the 1930s was the first study to demonstrate that paying attention to employees is a key motivator for increasing productivity. This experiment found that by fulfilling the factory workers' need to feel competent, achieve results, and be affiliated with a group, the workers actually became more motivated in their work. Subsequent studies have replicated the experiment's findings across other industries and professions, making clear the universality of how the human factor needs to be addressed in organizations in order for employees to feel motivated.

SELF-DETERMINATION THEORY

Thanks to new research in the positive psychology field—a vibrant branch in today's social sciences—motivation has been studied based on the principle that individuals are self-determined and more or less connected with their environment and engaged in it.

If our behavior is a function of who we are and our environment, we can express it as the following equation:

$$M = f(P,E)$$

Our Motivation (M) comes as a function of something internal to us, the person (P), and something external, from the Environment (E).

Our behavior and motivation are interrelated; each is inextricably linked to the other. How we are motivated—or at a minimum, the part of our personality that relates to how we act and our emotions—can be derived from the same measurements.

How we are motivated internally along with our most at-ease behaviors is reflected in our most natural way of behaving. What intrinsically motivates us is a result of our unique set of experiences, what we value, and what we need to be recognized for.

Motivation can also come from the outside, but—though we may perceive and internalize them—we will often feel a disconnect with extrinsic motivations, versus what naturally and intrinsically compels us to act.

Being extrinsically motivated requires acting differently than our most natural, intrinsic dispositions. Adapting our behavior with the appropriate incentives and support can be done in a way that is engaging. However, when adaptation is sustained for a long period and is too distant from our intrinsic motivation, it may cause us to disengage and be less productive.

INTRINSIC MOTIVATION AND FLOW

The concept of flow extends the notion of intrinsic or internal motivation to a state of satisfaction, engagement, contentment, and well-being that transcends one's immediate condition. Mihaly Csikszentmihalyi first formulated the notion of flow in this context, affirming that "happiness" does not adequately describe the state of contentment and fulfillment of purpose and meaning that one may find in life; this fulfillment is better encompassed by the concept of flow.

Still, the challenge remains to figure out how we can experience flow in our unique fashion, especially in the work environment. The GRI profiles provide a unique solution, with a clear distinction between the internal motivators that trigger flow and the external ones that distance us from it.

How we experience a state of contentment and flow varies according to our Natural behavior profile and its four factors that reflect how we perform in our job, are driven and motivated to act, along with how we experience positive emotions while performing in our own specific way. As we will see in Part II, learning the factor interactions and the behavior profile provides an even more nuanced snapshot.

A state of flow is more difficult to reach in organizations that exert undue pressure on us. A sudden shift in the market, the need for instant reorganization, or the loss of a major client prompt everyone to take on different roles immediately—roles that probably do not match our state of flow.

More simply, having to take on different behaviors in a job, even temporarily for an internship, switch to a new position, or stay in a position we dislike forces us to act away from our flow state of contentment and optimum performance.

External motivation can prompt adaptation, or conversely, a desire to find balance with after-work activities or a shift to a more adequate position in the future, possibilities that we will more fully introduce below.

ENGAGEMENT: THE IMPACT OF ENVIRONMENTAL EXPECTATIONS

When we use the word "environment," it encompasses more than what we might ordinarily perceive. The environment we attempt to adapt to is typically the work environment, which is populated by leaders and managers, direct reports, team members, and coworkers.

For an employee, the environment is generally dictated by the expectations and responsibilities of that person's actual position. For a potential candidate, it is the position they currently hold not the one they are applying for. If a candidate is not currently employed, then it's the environment where they are seeking employment.

The environment includes close relatives, coaches, mentors, or leaders who influence our perception and our need to adapt. These environmental influences reach us through direct contact or indirectly through media exposure such as reading, listening to podcasts, and watching videos.

Additionally, the environment may include people and experiences from the past, not just influences that are present. Typical examples of influencers who remain in our minds and influence the way we adapt are our parents and teachers.

So when our organization influences us to change our behavior, it is our perception of our environment and how we need to perform in it that is being affected, i.e., the expectations of how we should behave. As our perception of our role changes, so does the way we effectively behave.

> Being able to effectively influence an employee's behavior
> and performance requires understanding the person's
> intrinsic motivation, which is revealed by their most spon-
> taneous and natural way of performing.

Whether adaptation is appropriate or not needs to be viewed from
the perspective of both the employee and the organization, and
each party's capacity and willingness to find a middle ground.

How we perceive the needs of, and are motivated to adapt to, our
environment is likely to change over time. When we work to change
our behavior by training, coaching, mentoring, or various management techniques, it's our perception of the need for us to change
rather than our most natural way of behaving that is motivating
us. As our perception of the need for change evolves, our effective
behavior will change.

> Adaptation is generally necessary for short periods. Strong
> adaptation may be required for transitional periods. When
> adaptation is prolonged, it shows up in the role we perceive
> the need to act out, and eventually forces us to compensate
> and cope with the adaptation in various ways.

High adaptation, as we can measure it from a behavioral and emotional standpoint, will cause a decrease in productivity and an increase
in fatigue and stress that will be echoed in our engagement level.

How we interact with the environment not only determines how
we adapt, but also how more or less engaged we are. Engagement
is a sign of adequate stimulation from the work environment.
Conversely, low engagement signals a lack of adequate stimulation.

Engagement is closely connected with motivation. Once a lack of engagement has been detected and validated, it is most often appropriate to provide solutions to reengage a team member. In order to do that, what intrinsically motivates an individual's natural way of behaving must be considered on one side, and what is required by the environment of the job on the other side.

Positive communication, alignment with our most natural way of behaving, encouragement of our intrinsic motivations, and increasing the amount of appreciation, feedback, and incentives all positively affect our engagement level. Often, slight adjustments to job requirements or a better balance of activities outside work can have an instantaneous impact on the engagement level.

EFFECTIVE BEHAVIORS

Our effective behaviors are those behaviors that are most likely perceived by others. This results from combining how we naturally perform with our perception of the need to adapt to the environment.

Our effective behaviors may match the expectations others have of us and our efforts to deliver adequately. Adaptation is appropriate and necessary when we try to consciously deliver the outcome expected of us.

The behaviors required in a position can be defined through a behavior profile. By defining the specific behaviors required for a position within the organization, we can provide insight into the level of adaptation required of any given employee or candidate being considered for the position. Such an assessment can reveal how much organizational support will be needed in order for the person, given their natural way of behaving, to succeed in the position.

THE WHY BEHIND HOW PEOPLE PERFORM

Truly interpreting how people perform requires a more precise knowledge of how they naturally express their behaviors, how they perceive the need to adapt to their environment, and how that translates into effective, intrinsically motivated behavior and high engagement.

A role that is perceived to be aligned with an individual's natural behavior reveals a situation where they are in sync with their environment and acting in a way that suits their most natural disposition and expresses their core competencies and skills.

A lack of both engagement and alignment between natural behavior and the perceived role leads to ineffectiveness. The more distant these two components are, and the longer we stay this way without support from the environment or a rebalancing of activities, the less effective we are likely to become in our job.

> Choosing to place employees in roles that are aligned with their natural way of performing or making a point of providing the support they need to adapt to their role will ultimately improve individual and organizational performance.

With this knowledge, we can more effectively create environments where each team member is able to maximize their intrinsic motivation in the medium or long term, and receive the appropriate recognition and support to continue to grow, be motivated, engage with the work, and be productive.

The GRI behavior profiles were developed with the awareness that people can be productive and successful at their jobs in many different ways, often in ways that are distant from our own. Results can be attained differently; goals can be set, reviewed, and attained differently as well. The same is true for how each of us is motivated and engaged.

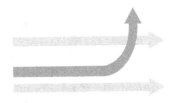

Chapter 5

METHODS FOR COLLECTING RELIABLE DATA

Similar to the early days of aviation, it took decades to conceive and build cars that can reliably take us from one place to another; the same is true for personality assessments. Cars today have developed to the point where we can get in without questioning whether the vehicle will actually work or if we will reach our destination. However, trust in the validity of personality assessments, which measure the intangible aspects of a person's character and behavior, has not always been a given.

In fact, there are so many different systems and methods for dissecting personality that it can be hard to discern the worthwhile from the frivolous. Is it surprising that people still turn to astrology, tealeaf reading, morphopsychology, and numerology to decipher human behavior?

When we assess personality, it's important to distinguish between what we measure and how we measure it. With the talent patchwork, we consider important characteristics of our personality. Each characteristic may be assessed by different methods and techniques. For the behavioral/emotional characteristic that we bring into focus with the GRI, the techniques listed below have been used over the years.

- *Structured behavioral interviews:* the person is probed for factual evidences on their behavior
- *Group interviews:* the person faces several interviewers at the same time
- *360-degree feedback:* the person is assessed on several traits by colleagues or others who happen to know them well
- *Assessment centers:* the person is assessed through a combination of multiple evaluations, including job-related simulations, interviews, surveys, and involving several assessors
- *Reference checks:* the person's previous accomplishments are checked by those who worked them
- *Surveys:* the person answers questions about their behavior, skills, knowledge, or previous experiences

Other common techniques, such as resumes, biodata, or work samples, are more appropriate for assessing skills, interests, or experience, but are not appropriate for assessing the behavioral/ emotional characteristic.

Among all the solutions, the survey technique emerges as the most efficient method for collecting and obtaining information on our personalities.

THE SURVEY TECHNIQUE

Surveys range from a series of questions to evaluating images of different forms like inkblots and words or reacting to realistic simulations. With the advent of the Internet and mobile devices, new scoring methods have emerged and questionnaires can now easily adapt to the participants' responses in real time.

In most cases, personality surveys require just a few minutes to complete or at most several hours. They are usually auto-administered—that is, individuals answer the questions themselves in isolation, rather than being interviewed by one or several people. Participants are allowed to read the questions in their own voice and with their experiences in mind.

The advantage of this is that the interviewer does not intervene in the process, and that person's suggestions or biases do not affect the outcome. The participant is away from the immediate and direct influence of assessors and the external environment. In this respect, the survey is said to be an objective technique.

In contrast, subjective techniques—such as interviews and 360-degree feedback—are inherently prone to the unconscious bias of the interviewers or assessors.

The survey technique is effective at collecting information quickly ahead of time so that the results can be used with other techniques such as interviews or assessment centers. It allows us to compare results, apply statistics, and, as a result, obtain more meaningful information.

Unlike other techniques, surveys are able to relate answers to a much larger number of participants, who represent the global population or one of its segments, by applying sophisticated statistics.

Surveys for assessing intelligence were the first type of survey to appear at the beginning of the twentieth century, establishing the standards for other types of surveys. Soon after came more specific surveys for measuring cognitive abilities, aptitudes, and competencies. Personality or behavioral surveys have had a long track record too, starting at about the same period. As with all other techniques, surveys are subject to standards of validity, reliability, potential adverse impact on gender, age or culture, and usefulness.

Thanks to the survey technique, as deployed through the GRI, we can assess the behavioral/emotional characteristic, or how people behave, in a way that cannot be assessed with other techniques.

STANDING IN OTHER PEOPLE'S SHOES

The survey technique also allows us to acknowledge how people perform from their standpoint. This information may compete with the first impressions we have of a person and may even feel counterintuitive at first.

Up through the 1990s, recruiters collected data about candidates' or employees' personalities with questionnaires or tests. The information yielded was of a clinical nature. Indeed, the surveys used were initially intended for clinical applications, and recruiters using them were required to be certified psychologists. The idea that this information could be work-related was questionable. For this reason, the results were kept confidential with psychologists.

But times have changed. Personal data that is in the normal range of behavior and is potentially work-related rather than clinical is available to anyone on the Internet. Information that is objective and reliable can dramatically assist us and any individual, including recruiters and executives, in our organizations.

Once available, the new data that comes from the assessment needs to first be understood and trusted. Then it can be further applied in multiple situations, and we can avoid the negative traps and the major impediments of our intuition and biases. We can start to appreciate individuals based on how they are intrinsically motivated to grow and perform.

THE SIMPLICITY OF TWO QUESTIONS

As noted previously, traditional ways of measuring personality focus on traits and types, which have different meanings depending on cultural context, education, background, and experience. Relying on a system that categorizes people by traits or types generates inaccuracies and leads to unconscious bias. For this reason, we designed the GRI to assess personality dimensions, also called factors.

We designed the GRI survey by using an adjective format and by measuring how someone perceives their own adaptation to the workplace environment and others' expectations of them.

The same adjective format that we use has been adopted by a limited number of personality assessments since the 1940s, starting with the pioneering work of Walter Clarke, an American psychologist and entrepreneur from Pittsburgh, Pennsylvania. It has proven effective for measuring the limited behavioral dimensions we wanted to assess. We have since refined and updated the process with recent findings and statistics from our research.

As a result, we have created a process that is simple and quick, yet capable of generating accurate and powerful personality measurements. Collecting data and creating an individual's GRI profile happens almost instantly. The assessment usually takes between five and fifteen minutes to complete and asks two questions.

Participants respond to each question by checking or not checking adjectives from a list. That's it. The process works the same in more than twenty languages the survey has been translated into.

The GRI survey has two universal questions: the first question is about your environment and what you believe is expected of you; the second question is about yourself and basically who you think you are. The survey's simplicity can be deceptive—but it is not simplistic. Complex data analysis goes on behind the scenes, which is further demonstrated by the depth and nuance of the results the survey yields.

The survey works in several ways. The most obvious benefit is that it allows people to answer the questions by creating their own narrative. No scenarios or contexts are provided. Instead, respondents are influenced solely by the two questions and by the context of how they are invited to take the survey (e.g., by an employer, as part of an employment interview process, by a friend or relative, etc.). This empowers people to respond with their own scenarios of how they believe they perform and how they believe others expect them to perform.

Because the GRI survey allows respondents to check as many or as few words as they want, the assessment is said to be open-choice. Other, forced-choice techniques ask participants to provide answers no matter what.

The results of the assessment are calculated using algorithms that translate the words checked and not checked into a specific GRI profile. Years of experience interpreting these profiles allow us to transfer the knowledge and benefits of the GRI to our users and clients.

The same measurements apply to various jobs and teams, enabling us to make comparisons when evaluating candidates and managing employees, as well as anticipating the support they will need in order to perform and succeed in their roles.

The measurements that result from this process may challenge the intuitive perception we have of someone, but will provide objective measurements and an objective language for discussing people, their jobs, and the organization.

ADAPTIVE BEHAVIORS

The GRI survey was devised to help business leaders apprehend individual adaptive behaviors, intrinsic motivation from a behavioral standpoint, and how people set their goals and grow more accurately with actionable data.

Although we may be curious about the cultural, biological, neurological, and historical reasons and the environmental or individual origins behind some behaviors, we know that some behaviors will be expressed more frequently and naturally than others, whatever the reason behind them. These rather regular and natural behaviors that are a part of who we are, are expressed through feelings and emotions. They are malleable and adaptable to some degree, and differently so for each of us.

However, portraying our personality as the proclivity toward certain kinds of behaviors is not as simple as categorizing a person's traits, which stick to them persistently and unchanged. We know that people adapt to their environment, are stimulated or not by the tasks they are asked to do, and eventually grow and evolve. How we behave is tied up with how we are motivated and engaged, and how we are driven to set and re-set our goals.

As we saw in Chapter 3, employers have to understand personality dimensions in a probabilistic way: How will someone most likely behave in a specific situation? How does their environment affect them? Does it engage and stimulate them emotionally? Then we need to flip this strategy around and be cognizant of how *we expect* someone to behave in a specific situation, e.g., a position within an organization.

PART II

THE
POWER
OF A
VISUAL
LANGUAGE

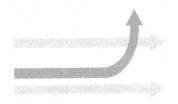

Chapter 6

A BETTER WAY TO PORTRAY PERFORMANCE

One of the important findings from the research on personality systems and other assessment techniques is that the words and expressions—as well as the concepts and theories they stand for—that we use to describe and make decisions about people are subjective.

We cannot stress this enough.

Words can have various connotations and overlapping meanings. Each of us interprets and makes use of them differently. There is no chance we can get close to a consensus when it comes to words or labels for describing personality. There are plenty of empirical reasons why they should not be trusted. For example:

- The same word or label may be attributed to two concepts in psychology that are quite different.

- Two concepts that have different labels may in fact be the same.

For instance, some techniques may assess "taking risks" and "being entrepreneurial," displaying these two phrases as distinct concepts—which they are—and providing different explanations for both in this respect. In fact, the two concepts being assessed echo the same underlying tendency, with slight nuances that have nothing to do with taking risks or being entrepreneurial.

Therefore, words have an inherent imprecision; they are naturally ambiguous, culturally biased, and impractical. This same imprecision carries over when we attempt to describe the personality traits, types, and behaviors expected at an organization.

Those who have traveled the world and worked in other countries have experienced how much humans are influenced by the concepts and theories of the culture in which we live. Whether or not we agree with our culture's current concepts and theories, they are ingrained in us. As we saw in Chapter 2 with the talent patchwork, we make use of characteristics and knowledge that shape these cultural theories.

The same challenges apply to how organizations deal with behavior. How certain kinds of behaviors are represented, encouraged, or suppressed become part of an organization's culture and all its artifacts—including recruiting, promotion, compensation, reward and benefit systems and even its perks. They influence how we assess people, think, judge, and make decisions about them.

THE GRI PROFILE

After individuals complete the GRI survey, the results are relayed via a GRI behavior profile that reflects their unique behavioral makeup and personality (see sample below).

Each profile is composed of four points and the lines that connect them. Each point represents one of the four core factors, which we describe in greater detail in the next chapter.

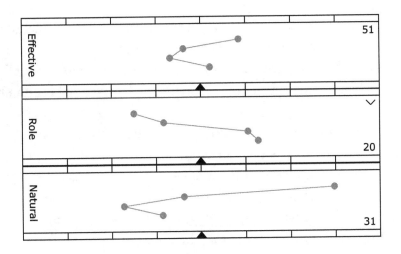

The profile can be viewed as a map that explains how a person behaves. As with maps, the profile depicts relatively permanent components that are essential for predicting future behavior, as well as components that are adaptive and may shift over time.

The GRI profile is not only predictive, but it can also be used to craft the behaviors needed for success in a position based on the combination of personality factors. Looking at several profiles at once can help organizations discern how a group of individuals will perform together as a team.

Before providing more details about the meaning of the four factors, let's first consider what each of the three graphs portrays.

THREE DISTINCT GRAPHS

The GRI behavior profile captures how we uniquely and naturally behave (the Natural). The profile informs us about how we adapt our behavior based on our perception of what the environment requires from us in order to perform appropriately (the Role).

The activity of perceiving, feeling, and thinking about the demands of our environment may translate into a different behavior than the one we naturally exhibit (the Effective). We may express ourselves differently when we are performing in a specific job than we would naturally.

When all three components of a GRI behavior profile are combined, they represent the full scope of a person's distinctive way of performing. However, the ingredients are not the same thing as the final product; a GRI profile represents more than the sum of its parts. Let's see what each of the graphs represent in more detail, starting from the one on the top, the Effective.

EFFECTIVE PERFORMANCE

The Effective profile is a visual representation of the behavior, motivation, and drive that is most likely to be observed of us at work or during job interviews.

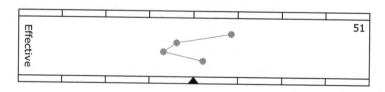

If our behavior matches the expectations that come from the organization, as a result of appropriate recruitment and management practices, this is the behavior to consider: the one that displays in observable facts, or the Effective.

Think about an actor who plays a role on stage or in front of cameras. What you observe from the outside is a combination of how the actor behaves naturally, modified by the role that person perceives the need to play.

PERCEIVED ROLE

The Role profile tells us about how we perceive the need to adapt to our environment. It is likely to change since it reflects our perception of our environment, which may change frequently over time.

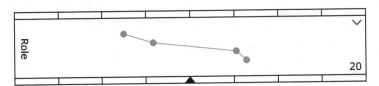

When we work to change our behavior through training, coaching, mentoring, or various management techniques, the perception of our need to change and the Role change too. As the Role changes, the Effective behavior will change too.

Adaptation as measured by the GRI is generally necessary for short periods. Strong adaptation may be required for transitional periods. When adaptation is prolonged, it shows up in the Role profile and requires some compensation mechanisms.

High adaptation will cause a decrease in productivity and an increase in fatigue and emotional labor as is evidenced with the Engagement Level represented by the arrow and number on the right.

NATURAL EXPRESSION

The Natural profile shows the behaviors, motivations, and drives that we more naturally and easily express. These are more likely to be displayed at home than at work or under stressful conditions when there is no time to adapt or act out a role. It is usually easier to validate and recognize people's Natural if we have known them for many years.

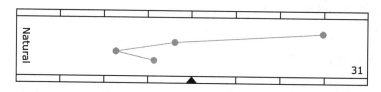

With the Natural, the four factors stay relatively stable over time. Their values may change slightly, but unlike the Role profile, the overall shape of the Natural profile remains consistent. In other words, it is highly unlikely that a factor will shift from one extreme on the continuum to the other.

The behavior illustrated in the Natural is predictable and reliable; you can anticipate behaving similarly now and in the future. Thanks to the reliability of the Natural over time, we can describe and predict a person's behavior, motivations, and drive with more accuracy. When we know the work environment, it becomes easier to predict an individual's performance in it.

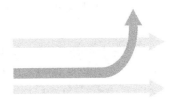

Chapter 7

THE FOUR FACTORS OF BEHAVIOR

The four factors are the basic components of a GRl profile. The three graphs, Effective, Role, and Natural, are built upon these four elements.

Each factor is represented in the profile by distinct dots. The lines connecting the dots create a unique visualization of how the four factors interact within an individual. The factors are measured along a scale in relation to the average.

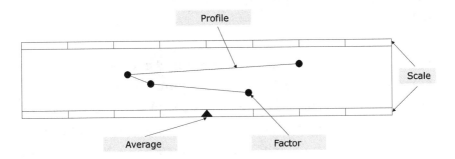

We made an intentional choice to label the factors with numbers instead of words. The four factors each represent multiple concepts with opposing meanings that are neither objectively good nor bad, so there is less chance of misunderstandings with numbers than with words. We refer to the factors as Factor 1, Factor 2, Factor 3, and Factor 4.

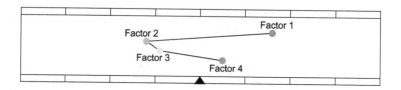

We identify the factors with colors. Red for Factor 1, green for Factor 2, yellow for Factor 3, and blue for Factor 4. The color code helps locate the factors visually in the profile. We make use of them in job profiles and for group analyses.

Each one of the four factors offers insight into a person's drive and motivation to perform in a certain way. As we briefly describe each factor, remember that none of them stands alone, but rather they influence each other; the understanding of one factor increases the depth and nuanced understanding of the others. Together, the four factors have more comprehensive meaning than each factor taken independently.

What is more, the four factors are universal and can be identified in individuals of any age, gender, or culture. These factors can be used to represent the behavioral requirements of a job at any level of an organization (the Position Behavior Indicator or PBI), and in the behavioral requirements of a team or company as a whole (the Team Behavior Indicator or TBI).

We will explain the content of each factor first, and then provide additional details about their scales in the next chapter. For now, readers should know that the big arrows and the characters displayed below are meant to inform on how each factor is expressed—more intensely at the poles of the spectrum on the right or the left, and less intensely when closer to a neutral position in the middle.

FACTOR 1

Factor 1 is presented at the top of the graph. When the factor appears on the high side (the right side of the scale) it shows that an individual needs and is motivated to **take command** of decisions and **dominate** in the environment, versus an individual who needs and is motivated to **be agreeable and modest,** when the factor appears on the low side (the left side of the scale).

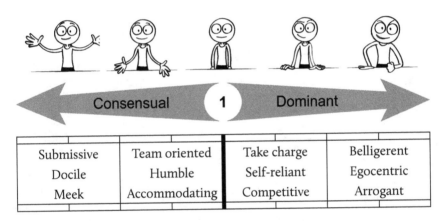

Submissive	Team oriented	Take charge	Belligerent
Docile	Humble	Self-reliant	Egocentric
Meek	Accommodating	Competitive	Arrogant

Factor 1 on the low side measures a low level or absence of need, drive, and motivation to confront others and dominate. Individuals with a low Factor 1 are more acquiescent and need to work in harmony. People with an extremely low 1 tend to be meek and submissive. Low 1s are naturally collaborative and attentive to others' needs with support and encouragement. They are friendly and hospitable.

Factor 1 on the high side measures a need, drive, and motivation to dominate and take command of decisions made in the environment. People with a high 1 act individually and exert authority without need of consensus. The higher the Factor 1, the more adventurous the person will be, and the greater the need to exert authority and take on new challenges. High 1s are naturally decisive, determined, and ambitious, taking responsibility for their own decisions.

FACTOR 2

Factor 2 on the high side shows that an individual needs and is motivated to **socialize and be in contact with people**, versus an individual who needs and is motivated to **be remote and analytically distant** when the factor displays on the low side.

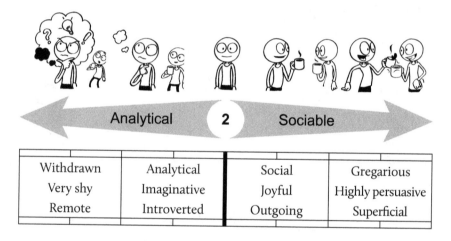

Withdrawn	Analytical	Social	Gregarious
Very shy	Imaginative	Joyful	Highly persuasive
Remote	Introverted	Outgoing	Superficial

Factor 2 on the low side measures the need, drive, and motivation to be involved in the technical, data-driven, tangible, and logical aspects of a task. A very Low 2 has little need to interact and will frequently withdraw from social activities. Low 2s are adept at organizing ideas and thoughts, and will take the time to critically evaluate them.

Factor 2 on the high side measures the need, drive, and motivation to socialize and be in contact with others. The higher the Factor 2, the more social activity is involved and the more outgoing the person is. A very High 2 may even be perceived as gregarious and superficial. High 2s have an accessible approach that enables them to accomplish things through others by collaboration and shared responsibilities. High 2s easily empathize with others.

FACTOR 3

Factor 3 on the high side shows that an individual needs and is motivated to **be in a calm and methodical environment**, versus an individual who needs and is motivated to **be free to change priorities and be spontaneous** when the factor displays on the low side.

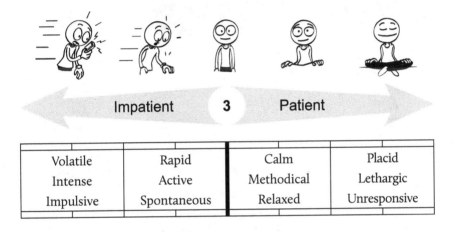

Impatient		3	Patient	

Volatile	Rapid	Calm	Placid
Intense	Active	Methodical	Lethargic
Impulsive	Spontaneous	Relaxed	Unresponsive

Factor 3 on the low side measures the need, drive, and motivation to be active and under tension, while constantly changing the pace of activities. An extremely low intensity of Factor 3 will drive the person to act impulsively. Low 3s seek fast, ready answers, decisions, and solutions while spontaneously responding to others.

Factor 3 on the high side measures the need and motivation to be stable, calm, tranquil, composed, and in a predictable environment. The higher the Factor 3, the more steady the person is. A very High 3 may even result in the person looking unresponsive. High 3s are cautious and careful, planning with a systematic approach.

FACTOR 4

Factor 4 on the high side shows that an individual needs and is motivated to **be formal and follow the rules**, versus an individual who needs and is motivated to **be informal and casual** when the factor displays on the low side.

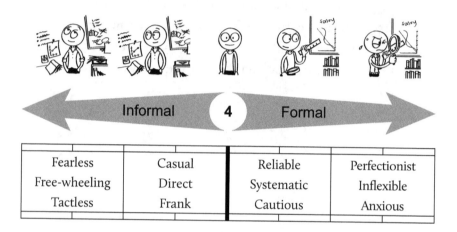

Fearless	Casual	Reliable	Perfectionist
Free-wheeling	Direct	Systematic	Inflexible
Tactless	Frank	Cautious	Anxious

Factor 4 on the low side reveals an absence of need, drive, and motivation to follow the rules. Individuals with a low Factor 4 are less sensitive to, or are fearless of, the eventual negative consequences of what they do, say, or decide. People with an extremely low Factor 4 tend to remain obstinately outside the norms of their environment. Low 4s do not tend to worry, are confident with uncertainty and risk, and rely on their own wit and experience. They remain positive in the face of perceived rejections.

Factor 4 on the high side measures a need and motivation to comply with rules. Individuals with a high Factor 4 tend to act in accordance with rules and standards. They are more sensitive to the consequences of what they do, say, and the decisions they make. When Factor 4 is even higher, every task is undertaken with extreme caution.

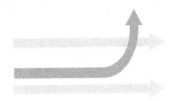

Chapter 8

THE FULL SPECTRUM OF
THE BEHAVIOR PROFILE

Each of the four factors is measured along a continuum that extends from the extreme low side (on the left) to the extreme high side (on the right). The distribution of the factors along the continuum follows a Gaussian distribution, also called the bell curve (see the figure below).

The bell curve is a simple way of bringing more accuracy to the measurement by looking at how probable it is that a particular factor will be expressed. It allows us to correctly account for the relative intensities of the factors within the profile when they are analyzed two by two or the four of them altogether.

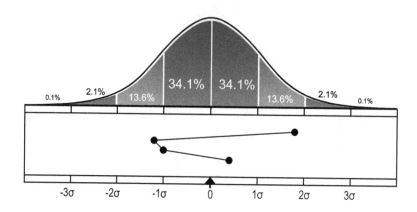

The **scale** is marked above and below the profiles. Each interval of the scale is a standard deviation (SD) or sigma (σ). The sigma scale provides an accurate measurement of a factor's intensity.

The statistics inform us that 68.2 percent of the population stands within 1σ around the average, 95.5 percent within 2σ, and 99.7 percent within 3σ. Very few people, 0.3 percent, have a factor beyond 3σ on both the low and high sides.

The **average** is represented by a triangle at the bottom center of each profile and allows us to compare each factor with the overall population. We say that a factor is **low** when it shows to the left of the average, and **high** when it shows to its right. Because "left" and "right" bear political connotations, we chose the language of statistics for this. However, making use of "low" or "high" is a linguistic convention. Having a factor on the high side is not better than having it on the low side. A profile will always have factors on the two sides; by design, the factors cannot be solely on one side.

FACTOR INTENSITY

The **intensity** of each factor is read by its distance from the average, either to the low or high side. The more distant the factor is, the more frequent, probable, and intense the expression of its corresponding behavioral strength and motivation, and the more noticeable and evident it will be.

By measuring the intensity, we can develop a more nuanced reading of a specific factor.

> A factor's intensity tells us how much energy it will take to behave in a way that expresses a factor further away on the continuum.

We talk about how intense a factor is by expressing its distance from the average in the standard deviation (SD) scale, or we use the language of statistics, by saying that the factor is **moderately**, **very**, or **extremely** intense on the low or high side. See how the scale corresponds below.

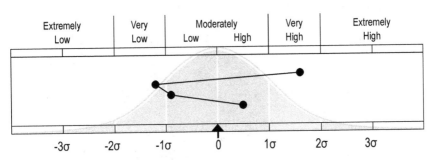

VISIBILITY OF BEHAVIOR

The two factors that we consider first when analyzing a profile are the two most distant; that is, the lowest and highest factors in a profile. The **visibility** of a profile is expressed by the distance that separates the two most remote factors. This value is calculated by counting the number of standard deviations between them.

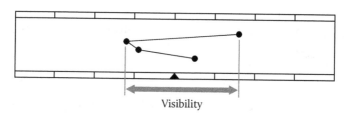

Visibility

The wider the profile, the more intensely and visibly the person will exhibit the corresponding behavior and motivation. The wider the profile, the easier it is to guess who the person is during interviews or at work, and the more of an impact the person will have on the environment through their two most extreme factors.

The narrower the profile, the less noticeable and intense the behavior is. When a person's factors are closer together, it is harder to guess who the person is based on interactions with them.

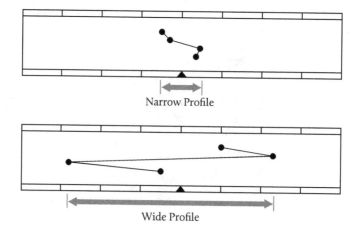

Narrow Profile

Wide Profile

People adapt and change. So too, to a certain extent, do people's behavior factors and their GRI profiles. But the wider the profile, the less likely it is that the factors will move to the other side of the average because it will take more energy to do so. The narrower the profile, the more the factors will evolve across and close to the average, yet the less likely it is that they will reach extremely low or high positions.

Some profiles may display the factors almost on top of each other, all located close to the average, as shown in the profile below. In this case, no single factor has any intensity; specific behaviors are difficult to identify and observe.

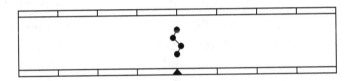

There is no situation that is right or wrong, no perfect profile visibility, and we observe people who perform well with profiles of all widths.

FACTOR INTERACTION

Imagine baking a cake. You have the recipe, which lists the individual ingredients—water, eggs, flour, and sugar—elements that are pretty straightforward by themselves. But put them together and apply heat and you end up with something else entirely: something with a flavor and texture distinctly different from its individual ingredients. We get a similar effect when the four factors are brought together to create a GRI profile.

Using factor interaction, we can consider the factors in pairs: Factor 1 with Factor 2, Factor 1 with Factor 3, and so on. There are a total of six combinations. Analyzing factor interactions is beyond the scope of this book, but here is what we can say about it in short:

- By themselves, each of the four factors has a meaning; at the same time, each factor influences the three other factors.

- When you look at factors in pairs, they reveal even more insights.

- The analysis of how the factors interact brings a fuller, richer appreciation of an individual's personality and predicts behavior and motivation with more accuracy.

People and their personalities and behaviors are complex and varied. Analysis of factor interaction is one of the ways that the GRI acknowledges this, adding more nuance to the profiles.

REFERENCE PROFILES

Looking at the whole profile, formed by the four factors connected by lines, brings more detailed information about the overall behavior, motivation, and drive of a person, than looking at the factors individually or two by two with the factor interactions. Each factor is refined by the understanding of the three other factors.

> There are an almost unlimited number of factor combinations and profiles of many shapes and widths—around sixty-three *billion*.

We created twelve reference profiles to offer a first, quick reading by considering the **shape of a profile**. Though no GRI profile is exactly like one of the reference profiles, the whole range of possible shapes is approximated through the twelve reference profiles.

Our individual GRI profiles are unique, as are the profiles of our boss, our spouse, and our team members. But an individual GRI profile is always closer to one of the twelve reference profiles than to the others, and offers us a general overview of—or introduction to—our likely behaviors.

The reference profiles have labels that help us talk more concisely about the general behavior and motivation exhibited by a person, instead of speaking about every single factor and their interactions. We may then talk about a Formal, referring to the Formal reference profile (see below).

We warned earlier about the ambiguous meaning of words; we again caution readers to use the twelve reference profile labels with care.

> We must be careful not to use the reference profiles to pigeonhole people in boxes or to limit them. Reference profiles can be used as an introduction to behavior and should be followed with a more nuanced reading of each individual profile.

When developing positions within organizations, these reference profiles help refine our awareness of the behaviors that are needed, making use of the profile shapes to better contrast the position's and team's requirements or to compare with individual profiles.

The following is an overview of the twelve reference profiles with their labels and a brief explanation of what they mean.

PROFILE	OVERVIEW
Dominant	• Self-directed and driven to fast action. • Competitive and ambitious determination, comfortable with pressure and speed. • Proactively initiates change, and assumes consequences.
Scientific	• Maintains real control of authority while being task-directed. • Exercises critical and creative thinking. • Focuses on problem solving from a rational and data perspective.
Creative	• Self-determined with personal resolve and little regard for risk or authority. • Prefers an unstructured environment. • Naturally comes up with innovative ideas, thinking outside the box.
Social	• Sociable with a gregarious, relaxed, and open behavior and natural expression of cordiality. • Communicates persuasively, with zeal and warmth. • Easily delegates authority and details.
Cooperative	• Congenial and warm. Empathizes and focuses on others' needs. • Cooperates within a team setting. • Shares and delegates with a friendly, amiable way and no self-interest.

PROFILE	OVERVIEW
Altruistic	• Fluent. Quick to connect to people. • Talks fast, with enthusiasm and an optimistic style of expression. • Persuasive and motivating. • Stimulates and communicates positively.
Patient	• Comfortable with recurring and repetitive work. • Acts patiently and modestly. • Calm and accepting. • Steadfast and reliable with a cooperative approach.
Supportive	• Systematic to change opinions and alter a viewpoint. • Open to new rules, plans and structure. Free to delegate the details. • Patient and steady on decision-making. A persistent approach.
Determined	• Reserved, quiet, and serious, particularly with unfamiliar people. • More comfortable and patient with the familiar. • Organizes and thinks before expressing herself/himself.
Formal	• Exacting in thought and communication. • Tends to be serious and restrained in groups. • Delivers careful, factual information. • Delegates cautiously with strong oversight to ensure quality.

PROFILE	OVERVIEW
Controlling	• Attentive to process and details. • Cautious about risks and mistakes. • Supervises with strong oversight to ensure quality control. Learns fast. • Wants to do things correctly and on time.
Courteous	• Compliant, agreeable, and considerate of the team. • Comfortable with the known and the givens. • Pays attention to details and processes. • Develops expertise. Does things right naturally.

Again, keep in mind that the reference profiles are provided here as an overview.[3]

Explanations, examples, and training are needed to become fully conversant with the profiles, build meaningful interpretations of them, and use them effectively for analyzing people, positions, and teams.

LEARNING A NEW LANGUAGE

As we pointed out in Chapter 2, our assessment and personal theories about people take more time to evolve, for example, than our adoption of new technology. It takes time to challenge and deconstruct our core beliefs and then reconstruct how we see the world

---

3 If you already have a GRI account and have taken the GRI Survey, you will find the reference profile that is the closest to yours under the tab **My Profile**. Profiles come with different intensities and many nuances that sometimes make it hard to identify the closest reference profile.

with new concepts. The theories we grow up with are reinforced by what we read and watch, and by the opinions of our parents, spouse, partner, friends, coworkers, and others we trust.

Even though more enlightened thinking, better decisions, and stronger relationships go hand in hand with new concepts that are more objective, our willingness to accept them and change is the same as it has been throughout our history: we make room for new concepts when we are challenged out of necessity. Just as the disciplines of math, biology, music, and computer programming have their own languages, we developed the GRI into a visual language for describing human characteristics.

GRI profiles rely not on words, but rather on visual representations—points and lines plotted on a graph—to describe an individual's natural behavior and unique way of adapting to environmental expectations. Reading a person's GRI profile is the first step toward unlocking their innate potential and ensuring they are in a position with the right amount of adaptation.

This approach helps to improve individual and organizational performance by providing neutral, actionable information about personality. If an individual's unique way of working can be revealed rapidly in a concise yet nuanced and visual representation, that information can then be applied in many situations to help us define job requirements more accurately and build better-performing organizations.

PART III

THE
PATH
TO
MASTERING
PERFORMANCE

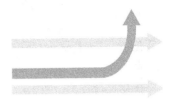

Chapter 9

CROSSING A TURBULENT STREAM

Once you have dramatically improved your understanding of how to assess and grow talent, what, then, is the best path forward to optimize your company's performance?

The business world is one that is constantly in flux. For this reason, the human aspects of any organization are often more intricate than anything else. Although marketing, sales, customer relationships, production, accounting, finance, etc., are becoming more automatized every day, all of these elements are managed or touched by human beings at some point. And the more employees experience turbulence with their projects, tasks, and relationships, the more turbulence the company will experience as a whole.

We have taken the seven following steps into consideration. Each of these will be explained and defined at great length in the following chapters:

- **Cultivate trusted relationships.**
- **Reinvent recruitment and management.**

- **Reduce friction and promote teamwork.**
- **Accept that success is not one size fits all.**
- **Define jobs with precision.**
- **Build teams more effectively.**
- **Design organizations that thrive.**

There is no hierarchy on a path made of stepping-stones, no specific order to follow but the one that makes the most sense to you and your business. Often one of these stepping-stones precedes all others: the potential friction or not-yet-discovered tension in an organization that is blocking performance. Such frictions end up being time-consuming and costly, and can be prevented. In other cases, it's recruitment that comes first because so much happens at that stage, such as the early impressions formed about candidates and the long-lasting consequential decisions made regarding those who then become the members of our organizations.

IDENTIFY EMPLOYEE INVOLVEMENT

Before you read about the seven steps, assuming you are in a company of more than one person, keep in mind that your organization's members also have their own views on each topic or stepping-stone.

The more employees you have, the more people there will be to discuss and express beliefs, concerns, and expectations about talent-related issues. Some will stay silent, while others will speak loudly; some may get organized, take on responsibilities, and influence or follow others' initiatives. They will use their own set of characteristics and techniques to assess individuals.

But having a common language to discuss and problem-solve in these seven areas can greatly benefit your organization, help reduce the turbulence of navigating the stream to success, and improve the performance of your employees.

WALK THE TALK

In the following chapters, we start with trust—one of the most important concepts for organizations to master in order to thrive and perform in the long term.

Once you have read about each of the seven stepping-stones, start with the one closest to your most pressing needs today. Then move to the next one and so on until you have made your way across all of them.

The last chapter of Part III will focus on learning about ourselves and others more quickly, and how the GRI system achieves that end. Learning about people faster can only happen within the context of your organization—a context that is complex, tumultuous, and in constant flux. The final chapter provides the best summary of the seven stepping-stones and how to continue learning about people rapidly and effectively.

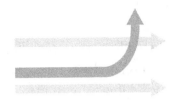

Chapter 10

CULTIVATE TRUSTED RELATIONSHIPS

Building trust may be one of the most important interpersonal elements in the workplace. Trusted relationships are usually developed over time and are the result of experiencing how people behave, but in work environments there isn't always time to build trust the traditional way, and the resulting ultra-condensed time-line can lead to miscommunications and costly errors.

For example, Linda was promoted to Director of Strategy and Marketing and has been reporting to the CEO, Joe, for the last six months. The two executives have many complementary interests, skills, experience, and concerns.

But they also work in very different ways. Performing doesn't mean the same thing for Linda that it does for Joe. After six months, Joe is having a hard time working with Linda, especially when discussing strategic issues, and he is not happy with her work. Everything Linda does is wrong. Joe decides to fire her.

This happened fast, and it wasn't handled well. It could cause problems for Linda, for Joe, and for the company.

Linda had tried to do her best and received a lot of support; being terminated was unexpected and a shock—she had no idea that she was doing something wrong. Having this on her record could create barriers to future employment and harm her career. She obviously can no longer count on a positive referral from Joe anymore.

For Joe, it weakened his leadership position. His teams felt that he made the wrong choice, that he should have been able to avoid the situation in the first place, and that he disrupted their workplace with the termination. Not to mention that they no longer trust him because they fear that they too could be terminated on a whim.

The company has suffered from wasted time, lost productivity, and wasted money: three months' delay on the project, one month of onboarding, and four months of training. The effect on the motivation, engagement, and performance of Linda's team and others was disastrous.

IT'S HARDER THAN EVER TO GET—AND KEEP—THE RIGHT PEOPLE

Grasping the chemistry of how people perform in teams is increasingly important. When dissatisfied with their relationship, people and companies can and do choose to go their separate ways. The temptation to look for better jobs on the Internet is just a click away. Thanks to new sourcing techniques, companies and their leaders have more options to easily reach out to new talent. Recruiters can find out about someone's potential faster than ever through easily accessible online resumes and AI-assisted robots that reach out to candidates.

With the advent of Glassdoor, Great Place to Work, Vault, and other websites that review what's going on inside companies, an organization's ability to engage and retain talent is now visible to everyone.

Dissatisfaction can no longer be hidden, and this leaves companies with no choice but to handle employee relations in a much more refined way than, say, even a decade ago.

As we observe in high-pressure environments such as Silicon Valley, people issues must be handled with care even when companies are moving at high speed. Better awareness of individual employee satisfaction and development enhances an organization's ability to perform effectively and grow faster.

Smart companies and leaders realize that lavish benefits and high salaries are not the only way to motivate. They realize that if they don't apply other methods to retain employees, their company can develop a bad reputation, dissuading other talent from joining the firm.

THE NEED FOR TRUSTED RELATIONSHIPS

For organizations to function efficiently, they must embrace the idea that trusted relationships in the workplace are vital to their success. Trust is one of the core values essential to productive teams and individuals. A high-trust environment is one where team members and their managers are engaged and productive.

The story of Linda and Joe is the story of trust—or lack of it—which leads us to the urgent questions facing every organization:

- How can trust and relationships between people be handled more effectively?

- How can our work experience be more fulfilling, before, during, and after the contractual relationship—through the engagement, retention, motivation, and separation process?

Look at these questions from the perspective of personal relationships, like life partners or parent-child relationships. A significant amount of empathy is needed to nurture such relationships. And as we all know from our own experiences, it may take years for a parent to fully understand his or her child, or for anyone to truly know their parents, siblings, spouse, or partner.

It even takes a lifetime for someone to really know who they themselves are, what drives and motivates them. It is no surprise, then, that building an efficient, trusted work relationship is challenging, just like it was for Joe and Linda.

A person cannot maintain a productive and rewarding relationship of trust through good and bad times, particularly when dealing with strong internal and external pressures, without actively developing a deeper comprehension of their own distinct way of performing and interacting with teammates.

HOW DO TRUSTED RELATIONSHIPS DEVELOP?

At work, as in our personal lives, trust is based on getting to know someone over time. With each experience we have of another's behavior, we add to our knowledge of them: are they reliable? Are they honest? Do they follow through?

And trust grows or fades.

A trusted relationship is based on confidence in capabilities—will my teammates perform competently?—and predictable behavior—will my coworker or manager act in an expected way most of the time?

However, trust doesn't always come naturally. The basic relationship between employees and their organizations can be written in black and white in signed contracts. These contracts define some basic foundations of trust: as your employer, I trust that you will show up at your starting time, stay the agreed-upon length of time, and do what you are asked.

But these contracts don't build any personal trust. As an employee, just because I sign a contract, that does not mean that I trust the organization to have my best interests at heart or that my team-mates will be reliable. The competencies and skills that people bring to the team are not enough by themselves to indicate how they will be used to benefit the team.

Organizations cannot rely on lip service alone if they truly want to reap the benefits of trust. With time at a premium in business, managers must find ways to be proactive in building trust quickly and before problems begin.

Manage Performance

To trust that a person will perform well in a job requires that expectations be communicated clearly and that team members find some meaning and purpose in the work.

- Matching a team member's behavior profile with job expectations removes the guesswork and lets us put the right person in the right job and handle the lack of fit when it exists.

- This creates both efficiency and trust with team members since we are helping them to better develop their abilities and skills.

Cultivate Diversity

Diversity of skills, experience, and style helps create an atmosphere of creativity and innovation, where differences in personality are consciously sought out and acknowledged.

- Detailed behavior profiles help team members clarify and manage differences by making sure that the whole team recognizes and accepts them sincerely, not superficially.

- Working through differences from the outset helps teams build trust and prevents problems from developing over time.

Improve Interaction and Increase Productivity

Each team member needs to understand the others and know how to work with everyone's talents. If teams ignore differences or allow one or two members to impose their style on the rest, the team will end up with unhappy members whose trust is shattered, to the detriment of the entire team and their work.

An individual's personality is an important factor in building trusted relationships. Teams are naturally at risk of losing trust and creating loose relationships due to the misinterpretation of behaviors and misguided expectations of others.

The key is to identify employee behaviors, needs, motivations, interests, and values by providing measurements for the workplace that are clear, positive, shareable, acknowledged, and consistent.

With greater knowledge of everyone's unique way of performing, we gain more confidence in predicting how we act and develop, and thus are better equipped to build trust, and consequently, a more productive, profitable organization.

DEVELOP THE PEOPLE SKILLS OF MANAGERS

Situations like Joe and Linda's can be avoided. Generally, a manager must take the initiative to improve the relationship. The manager needs to make sure that new team members are properly recruited and onboarded, that the teams are properly engaged, and that all their members are working together efficiently.

If Joe had had a clear grasp of Linda's intrinsic motivations, he very likely could have found a way to address his frustrations long before they became overwhelming.

Even in turnaround and conflict situations, the communication between employers and employees can be improved and mastered.

As one senior executive of a biotech industry in San Francisco puts it: "Getting the team dynamic right at the front end is one of the critical success factors to the outcome of the effort. It's actually one of the things that is hardest to do for managers because it requires a level of intuitive understanding that can take years to amass if you're working with people on a day-to-day basis. So getting that right early is honestly one of the biggest challenges that successful companies are capable of doing."

IT'S WORTH THE EFFORT

Cultivating strong people skills is at the heart of what it means to be a manager and build great, trusted relationships. These skills are certainly the hardest to develop, especially in a highly pressurized business environment; they also take the longest to cultivate. But because of the potentially huge benefits they offer, it's important for managers to develop trust quickly and be as objective and impartial as possible, rather than subjective and partial.

For Joe and Linda, it's too late. But all is not lost. Joe can do better when he chooses Linda's replacement, and he can improve his relationships with his current staff to regain his lost leadership credibility. In the future, if Joe becomes more enlightened about how people can be motivated to perform and succeed in their work, he can salvage his relationships and come out stronger and more effective. He can do all of this much faster than he would have if he had simply followed his own trial-and-error experiences.

In our modern, ultra-connected, fast-paced, and continually changing world, the relationships leaders and managers build with team members are a critical strategy for success.

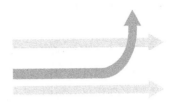

Chapter 11

REINVENT RECRUITMENT AND MANAGEMENT

One of the first benefits of deploying personality assessments like the GRI in companies is that it facilitates greater transparency about both people and the organization by transforming the recruitment and management process within a company.

Often we find that data is collected during recruitment, but the information is not passed on to management for the interview process or once candidates are hired and onboarded. Similar data may be collected later from the same employee for team-building and coaching activities or during performance review season when important decisions are made about promotions. This leads to an inefficient process that wastes people's time and doesn't take advantage of good, work-related information you have already collected about people.

On the contrary, data points should be collected not merely while recruiting and interviewing new candidates, but also in managing, coaching, promoting, and developing leadership potential in existing team members. Sharing and retaining the data from an employee's assessment allows organizations to streamline the recruitment and management process over the course of a person's entire career at a company.

Collecting more objective information ahead of recruitment and circulating it between recruiters and managers early on helps alleviate major obstacles that may come up once the candidate is hired and begins working. In addition, when this objective data is used in management and shared among an actual team, every team member can become better aware of their strengths and how they fit in with the strengths of their teammates.

In this chapter, we review how recruiters and managers can use behavioral data to improve the hiring process and how candidates and employees benefit from its use.

HIRING

When hiring new employees, we naturally tend to rely on our gut feelings or instinctive awareness about candidates. Instinct, while it can be useful and necessary in certain situations, is too subjective and easily affected by individual biases to be consistently effective in hiring. Instinct is honed over many years of experience, but even then, it is still neither objective nor sharable.

INTERVIEWING

The behavioral/emotional component of a job is the most difficult to assess with accuracy and objectivity, while the skills and experience necessary are relatively easy to identify. Referring to a candidate's assessment helps us tailor our approach and attitude toward the candidate in order to engage them quickly and genuinely during the interview.

Defining the behavioral requirements of a position in detail allows us to gauge how closely the candidate aligns with those requirements and choose questions that provide a fuller picture of the candidate and the job fit. This makes it easier to dig into their resume and ask questions that connect their behaviors, skills, and interests to the potential job.

> For instance, Paxton Song, COO of FuelX, said, "For the interviewing process, we were able to utilize the GRI's information by not only understanding what attributes in the candidate we were looking for, but to also identify specific questions and how the candidate would respond to those specific questions in order to identify and ensure that there was a solid fit for the position, as well as that person's natural abilities."

In a situation where we're selling the position to a candidate rather than screening them, knowing the candidate's profile helps present the job in the most positive light, while the job requirements clarify the behaviors that the candidate will need to develop in the new position.

ONBOARDING

There is no need to wait until problems surface to start building a great team. So often we just plug along until there are problems, and only then do we organize a retreat or a conflict-resolution workshop to fix them. The recurring expense of an ineffective team can be enormous.

Making wise and effective decisions about a team starts as early as the recruiting process, then the onboarding time can be used to learn about team members' differences and help the team work together more efficiently from day one.

When managers and team members are better aware of and appropriately educated about how they perform differently and the nature of their various positions, unnecessary frictions can be avoided and the team can be set on a better path for success. As always, the team's manager plays a critical role in this process.

MANAGING PEOPLE

At its most basic, better quality data and assessments of people provide managers with a unique method for understanding others more accurately so that they can recruit, interview, coach, and manage team members more efficiently. Such tools help managers navigate the expectations of the organization for all of its positions and relate them back to the individuals who occupy those positions and teams.

> Adrian Hall, the CEO of CF Engine, has found the GRI to be an important catalyst for more effective management at his company. Managers were able to look at the profiles of their team members and see "why Jim may get on with June or not and how they can maybe try and give an awareness to the team of why one individual isn't necessarily getting on with another individual in a particular team."

Since everything that is done within organizations is done through its people, clarity about what they do and how they do it should be the ultimate goal for organizations. It may come as no surprise that people management, which ideally ought to be more objective, precise, and scientific, tends to be more of an art based on gut feelings and subjectivity.

By learning about the behavioral profiles of team members and what is required of each of them, managers can manage their teams according to specific members' needs and the team's overall objective. Team members can determine the best way to communicate and work with each other, even in challenging times (such as during acquisitions or mergers).

How employees need to be handled through periods of change can be better informed and more successfully handled when organizations have access to quality data regarding the talent they already possess. This requires appropriate implementation by the organization's leaders and managers. People matters are sensitive by nature and have to be handled with care.

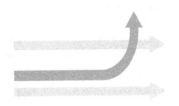

Chapter 12

REDUCE FRICTION AND PROMOTE TEAMWORK

There is a concept of friction in physics that broadly states that a small amount of friction can impede an object from working efficiently and an excess of friction can even prevent the object from working at all. An example of this: a car needs oil in its engine to run, without which the engine will quickly overheat, damage all of its components, and seize up.

In organizations, friction can occur between people, but there is no easy way to measure it as we do in physics.

A certain amount of friction within an organization is often inevitable and sometimes even desirable, like the friction we naturally experience when we learn new skills outside of our comfort zone. Other types of friction can't be avoided, such as when a machine breaks down during production, the Internet goes out of service, a client suddenly delays an order, or an employee gets sick and can't report for work.

But other organizational friction is directly influenced by the assumptions we make about the people in our organization. This kind of friction leads to a loss of engagement and productivity that ultimately impacts the bottom line negatively. It is unnecessary and can be prevented or resolved. This chapter discusses some common points of friction that we can identify and solve with assessment data.

MINIMIZE FRICTION BETWEEN TEAM MEMBERS

There are numerous reasons why two people might clash or fail to get along. Maybe they have a different education, cultural background, or family history, to name a few. Unconscious biases can also provoke disagreements.

Unfortunately, problems between team members are most often discussed too late when the friction has increased to a point of no return. Assessments can prevent major conflicts by explaining individual differences in behavioral/emotional characteristics and demonstrating that behavior is not related to gender, education, age, sexual orientation, or culture.

Training in unconscious bias facilitates the inclusion of all people at organizations, but it does not provide a more objective appreciation of their unique work-related characteristics. By focusing on behavioral characteristics and preferences as they relate to work, it becomes clear that everyone has a chance to succeed in their jobs if we are inclusive of their differences.

For George Northup, CEO of Author-IT, this meant revisiting the profiles of his executives to better understand how to work with them. "I'm always pressing our executives to go faster, to deliver more, and to go to a higher standard. And there have been points with either our CTO or CFO where I have felt a strange reaction, which in a vacuum I might have interpreted as resistance or perhaps a lack of buy-in to whatever I was trying to do," he said.

"My natural reaction would be to get angry or to get impatient, and to push harder or to perhaps punish these individuals. So, by going back to the data, it's a reminder that they're actually aligned with me in goals...what I might have interpreted as resistance is actually the methodology of how they approach things."

RESOLVE MISMATCHED HIRES

Friction can occur when a job requires behaviors that don't come naturally to us. A strong disconnect between a position's demands and our natural behavior can cause boredom, ineffectiveness, lack of creativity, and decrease of engagement.

This disconnect between the person and the job can often be solved by first acknowledging it, and then providing a remedy, such as a better balance between work and non-work activities, adjusting the position to match the person, or extra support and development for the employee so that they can cope with the job.

ALLEVIATE LANGUAGE BARRIERS

It can sometimes be difficult to find a common language when talking about people and their personalities. Not all words, concepts, and theories mean the same thing to everyone. This is especially true for describing the behavior required in a job. When we use data and judgment-free assessments to evaluate talent, we no longer have to rely on labels and categories that are inaccurate.

WITHHOLD JUDGMENT

Biases and gut feelings naturally limit our ability to understand others from their own perspective—to view the world from their shoes. We don't know what we don't know about people.

Some call these blind spots.

Both positive and negative emotions about people may creep into our decisions. In order to make better judgments, we need better information about people. When we realize that each person has a unique way of expressing themselves, we value their strengths and differences more. In the absence of this realization, there is frustration, reduced interest and motivation, and fewer successful relationships.

Knowing our own profiles and the profiles of others helps us to better distinguish the emotions involved in our interactions and make sense of their outcomes.

INCREASE SELF-AWARENESS

Lack of self-awareness is another potential source of friction. A more nuanced appreciation of our motivations increases our self-awareness and helps us anticipate areas where we might encounter friction. Better awareness of our strengths and motivations leads to better decisions for our career path.

> As an executive of Silicon Valley trained in the GRI put it this way: "Any tool that enables me to better understand how I'm wired and how I am likely to show up gives me an opportunity to decide how I go about doing it, so that I am at least as effective as I can be."

When we know who we are, we can better inform the people around us about how we need to be understood and supported.

ENHANCE GROUP PERFORMANCE

A company can be in the right market with a great product and great timing, but still experience terrible results. Maybe sales did not come through or a new technology was implemented too late. What went wrong? People are the easiest factor to blame when an organization underperforms.

Organizations have their own set of norms, rules, and processes embedded into their culture, which leaves everyone and no one in particular to blame except, ultimately, the CEO. The organization as a whole may not have hired the people it needed or managed them adequately in order to perform. Another friction that should be prevented.

As a result of not having the right people, targets are not met, start-ups fail to launch, and companies eventually close. Operating in competitive markets requires both thinking and acting fast, or at least faster than competitors. In less competitive markets, growing and surviving over the years requires paying attention to people more accurately, too.

How an organization performs as a whole and the people who make up the organization can only be analyzed in relationship to the market it competes in and how it sets, continually resets, executes, and meets its targets.

GET SMARTER ABOUT PEOPLE

We wish that years of experience were enough to learn about something so fundamental and basic as human nature. However, it remains one of the most elusive concepts in modern life.

Mastering how to hire for an organization's needs and learning what motivates people's intrinsic drives are happening at too slow a pace and too high a cost, which constitutes another friction that prevents the growth of individuals and companies.

Attending MBA programs and gaining years of experience in people management doesn't seem to expedite the learning curve of becoming proficient in people matters. The process remains hard, painful, and costly. Executive coaching and mentoring programs have helped. However, they are no substitute for the knowledge that managers and executives need to quickly develop in order to deal with people smartly, decisively, and on their own.

The concept of *emotional intelligence* was popularized by David Goleman's publication of the book of same name in the mid-1990s, bringing forward a new perspective that being smart about people has something to do with emotions rather than a higher IQ. Managing people is not about mastering political games or learning how to influence others. Those tactics are simply forms of extrinsic motivation.

Removing the friction around becoming astute about people requires new learning—an experience and training of a new nature—which, if successful, accelerates the process of improving our social intelligence.

REDUCE THE COST OF FRICTION

A common problem discussed in this chapter is how hard it is to identify forces of friction at first sight without a more objective assessment. In other words, you can relax until you start feeling the pain and it hurts the bottom line. You could hardly have prevented that friction without access to necessary information in the first place.

Various types of friction, however, translate into much that is unwelcome in a company, such as:

- Lack of interest and fulfillment
- Reduced creativity
- Unstable relationships between team members
- People who leave because of poor management practices
- Imprecise language that carries ineffective decisions
- Time wasted in interviews
- Hires that do not match the organization's needs
- Mentoring, training, and coaching support that fails to provide expected results
- Disengagement
- High employee turnover

KPIs in finance, production, marketing, service, etc., hardly capture the above intangible aspects of a job. The implementation of KPIs is an indicator itself of professional management, but it hides the behavioral/emotional characteristics at play that help to deliver those KPIs.

Friction eventually leads to disengagement and turnover in a company. A lack of creativity and innovation generates additional friction. When this happens, people frequently take action to leave and move to more rewarding positions and organizations.

By mastering the intangible aspects of managing people from an objective perspective and creating a culture that hires, welcomes, and rewards various ways of performing and succeeding, companies can remove friction that would have otherwise prevented them from enduring and growing.

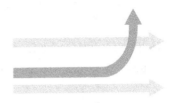

Chapter 13

ACCEPT THAT SUCCESS IS NOT
ONE SIZE FITS ALL

As much as we want companies to be professionally managed and follow a controlled and predictable growth path, more often they turn out to be like an aquarium where fish of various sizes and personalities have been thrown together in a close environment. Big fish quickly swallow the small ones, and the small but aggressive fish challenge the slow and docile ones. Soon there may not be any fish, colorful or otherwise, left at all.

Nasty political games can creep into organizations, as well as all sorts of friction as we saw in the preceding chapter, and prevent them from functioning efficiently. Competitors may enter the market and that will endanger the company's early successes. Mergers, splits, and other reorganizations will create anxiety and insecurity that may scare away some key employees.

For an organization to grow successfully, leaders must be ever vigilant of unexpected events from inside and outside the company.

Beginning with the leadership team, the organization will need to count on its people to adapt quickly and survive hard times.

By managing employees more effectively, a company can retain the leadership, creativity, and entrepreneurial spirit of its early successes that are needed for its future. It can better advance in uncharted territories and face the unexpected without delay.

In this chapter, we consider several ways that the GRI addresses core concepts in organizational development and can contribute to a company's continued prosperity.

REWARD ALL LEADERSHIP STYLES

There are as many ways of being successful as there are individuals! Being disruptive, radical, and a risk-taker can ultimately lead to success just as easily as being methodical, detail-oriented, organized, and structured.

Acknowledging that everyone has their unique way of achieving success and becoming a leader is the starting point for progress. Finding one's unique way and valuing it is no small affair. From our observations with the GRI, very few people come to this realization without hard work.

As we build our definition of what success means for each of us, we need to remember that our colleagues may have different definitions of performance and success. In fact, there are as many ways to lead as there are people on this planet.

There is no better way to demonstrate this than through four examples of leaders who have made their mark with very different styles. Below we examine each of their GRI profiles. We purposely chose these four leaders because they each represent a different quadrant in the standard grid.

The first profile shows a natural tendency to express authority and strong command, a desire to pursue the company's goals aggressively, and the ability to remain confident while facing resistance and the unforeseen.

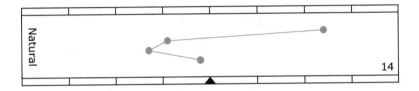

The closest reference profile is the Scientific; this profile, however, has a higher Factor 2 than the reference profile, which means this person will reach out to people more spontaneously, and a lower Factor 4, which makes this person more informal than the Scientific.

This individual founded a company that produced innovative cloud computing technologies, a disruptive go-to-market strategy, and high-speed growth. The company quickly attracted venture capital money, grew a team of talented individuals, became prominent in its market, and was later successfully sold to a competitor.

This second profile reveals an above-average tendency to network spontaneously and socialize confidently with new people, as well as a desire to influence others.

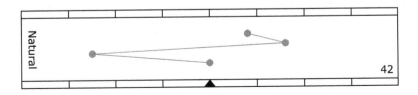

The closest reference profile is the Social, though this profile has a much higher Factor 4 that helps formalize follow-up and delegation when reaching out to contacts.

This leader has successfully flipped, funded, and scaled several companies by reaching out to investors and people with new ideas and emerging technologies in the tech industry. The complexity and details of execution are brought to fruition by the team, while the organization is managed by this fearless, audacious, and charismatic leader.

Profile three is closest to the Determined reference profile, which shows a patience and persistence to consistently push ahead for new and unconventional ideas.

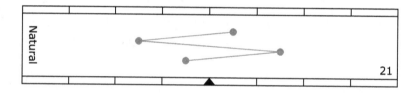

This person expresses radical creativity without fear of the bizarre or unfamiliar.

This particular individual has opened new paths by leading innovation in the open source programming space. This leader takes the time to think ahead and use his authority to consistently push forward new ideas, even when the people around him are resistant to change. Public speaking is not this leader's forte, so speaking opportunities are delegated to others in the company who excel at it.

The fourth profile is closest to the Formal reference profile, with a slightly lower Factor 1 and Factor 3, which translates into more spontaneity, cordiality, and openness to others' opinions.

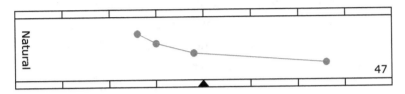

People with this profile scrupulously go through all the minutiae that is needed to deliver high-quality work.

This person developed a brilliant go-to-market approach that became highly successful in the microprocessor industry. The leader put forward an amazing strategy that others in the organization worked to implement. Delegation and follow-up is managed with rigor, and attention to detail and the needs of teammates provide expertise and sound advice.

When diversity in leadership styles is valued and exemplified by those at the top of the organization and ingrained in the company's culture, others have a better chance at experiencing leadership and growing their own leadership skills, too, as in the four examples above. A diversity in styles starts with a more objective selection of employees. It continues with mentoring, coaching, and other developmental programs where it needs to be proactively valued.

FOSTER CREATIVITY

Creativity is an important quality in business, most obviously in the development of new products and services, but also in how we finance development, sell and market products, and write and negotiate agreements. We have to be creative in order to better attract, reward, and motivate talent. Properly understood and implemented, creativity fuels a company's sustainability and growth.

Valuing creativity means being open to appreciation, communication, and attitudes that are disconnected from our own experience or cultural ways of looking at issues. Acceptance, humility, forgiveness, and openness help with this process.

Just like leadership, creativity comes in different flavors, too, as in the four profiles above.

- **With the first profile**, creativity comes with much assurance by thinking deeply, engineering and expressing the ideas with strong command. The person not only expresses new ideas, but also takes the initiative to implement them.

- **With the second profile**, creativity emerges thanks to discussions with people who naturally express themselves. Creative ideas flow from the network and get promoted to others.

- **With the third profile**, it's more about taking time to think and push forward unconventional ideas. The most radical ideas may emerge from this style.

- **As for the fourth profile**, creativity is embraced with an above-average capacity to master the details and refine ideas and sincerely assist with the follow-up.

Creativity is a process that needs to remain open to new ideas regardless of the style they are expressed and shared through; the most absurd suggestions from individuals who seem to be the most ludicrous often turn out to be the most precious. In organizations, the best creative ideas do not come from one person, but from a large pool of people who are part of or even outside of the organization. Smart minds borrow and build on others' ideas. They accept having their own mindset challenged and embrace keeping things loose for future ideas.

When you embrace the need for creative thinkers and recognize that there are many different ways to be creative, as we do with the GRI, the challenge will not be a lack of creative ideas, but a question of which ones to take to the next step in the innovation process.

ENCOURAGE RADICAL INNOVATION

Taking a disruptive, radical idea out to market requires persistence, continuous learning, and a focus on selling, organizing, and leading in tough times. One has to deal with uncertainty and constant rejections when engaged in this scenario.

Active support for radical innovation within an organization does not happen by chance either, and it isn't always easy. New ideas disturb established ideas, products, and markets.

Radical innovation produces friction.

Some people are not deterred by radical innovation. On the contrary, they relish the battle. The typical behavior profile for radical entrepreneurs has a very high 1, very low 3, and Factor 2 and Factor 4 in between them, close to the average—like the one below.

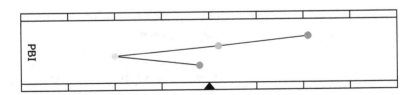

Leaders with this profile are naturally stimulated by challenging the status quo and initiating change with a strong sense of urgency. They innovate for the satisfaction of solving big problems and disturbing the conventional.

Since large organizations by nature have many rules and tend to avoid risk, they tend to scare away these radical entrepreneurs. Established companies tend to hire people who fit the culture, but are not necessarily a fit for high-speed innovation in highly competitive markets.

> Ruy Shiozawa, CEO of Great Places to Work in Brazil, shares the belief that organizations must create the right environment and internal structure for great ideas to surface. "There are many analyses that show for each great idea we have today, 400 other people are going to have the same idea in a short period of time. So innovation is not to do with having the idea," he explained. "Lots of people have great ideas all the time, but out of, let's say, one hundred ideas, just three will be implemented, and maybe one or two will be successful. So what is critical is the path from idea to execution."

Hubs for entrepreneurs and large companies interested in radical innovation need to not merely consider the birth of an idea, but also production, sales, and all the obstacles that will need to be cleared on the way to execution. Since these tasks will require different competencies and styles to excel and outperform the competition, leadership and management skills are called for.

Those who are more radically entrepreneurial should be free to think and act, yet also be held accountable for the resources invested in their projects. If we desire innovation, we cannot force structures and ideas upon entrepreneurs. Instead, we must let go of the reins and allow them to run free.

Radical innovation involves more than thinking smart and coming up with brilliant ideas. Another form of energy is required to take those ideas to market, pitch investors, involve teammates, and build an organization. Proactively adjusting a new product or service, its production, selling it, and scaling it in the market at high speed all rely on the behavioral/emotional characteristic of our talent patchwork that we need to master.

CULTIVATE A SUPPORTIVE ENVIRONMENT

Companies are composed of a mix of very different profiles. They have to be, since so many different tasks—production, accounting, sales, and client services—need to be performed in so many distinct ways.

A company leader's success never belongs to that person alone, but also to the amazing people who work with them. Competitive markets can be rough, requiring leaders to be confident and adopt a direct communication style. They may have to regularly face the new, risky, and unknown. Building a team that accepts and deals with these conditions is an important part of an organization's success.

For example, Lightbend, a technology company, has acquired a couple of small companies over the years, and in each case, CEO Mark Brewer wanted to ensure a smooth transition process and foster an environment where the new team felt welcomed and fully integrated. The new teams took the GRI Survey as part of their onboarding process. "They both saw the value in what it told them about themselves, but they also saw value in how they could learn or better understand how they were going to fit within Lightbend and the team members they would be working with," Mark said.

To attract, nurture, and grow talent for an organization, we first need to interpret people and their behavior more accurately. The best way to do this is by assessing the less obvious and most ubiquitous characteristics found in their behavioral/emotional profile. Assessments can quickly provide this information and offer insight on what to do to bring out the best in people.

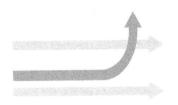

Chapter 14

DEFINE JOBS WITH PRECISION

In his best-selling book, *Good to Great*, Jim Collins considers what propels companies to succeed and arrives at this conclusion: running an organization is like driving a bus; the driver has to make sure the right people are on the bus in the right seats. That analogy, which has since become well known, challenges us to pay more attention not only to the leaders of companies, but also to individual team members and how they are each paired with the right job. This focus, however, does not change how difficult it is to distinguish which characteristics are needed to qualify a person for a specific job or match them with a specific team or manager.

Yet the hiring process often focuses solely on the prospective candidates and their patchwork of talents. Organizations must use data about their behavior to evaluate how responsibilities and skills should be expressed and developed for a specific position.

Why is it critical to look at the positions individuals take on and not merely the individuals themselves? Because if you want people to succeed in their positions in practice, not just in the abstract, you must examine what the position requires of them. That's what we typically do when we list the competencies expected in a job. We assume we will find candidates with matching competencies.

As you saw in Part 1, behavioral/emotional characteristics do not adapt at will. When the behavioral requirements of a position are too distant from an individual's natural behavior, this leads to unnecessary tension, lack of motivation and flow, disengagement, and finally, underperformance.

For that reason, a more refined understanding of the behavioral/emotional demand in a given position helps to better anticipate the corresponding characteristics needed in prospective candidates and the assistance that individuals may need to adjust if their profile is not an ideal match for the position.

Focusing on positions rather than on their occupants has proven to be a powerful way of engaging strategic discussions on what may be missing in an organization at any level, how to attract and keep the best talent, and when to open jobs for candidates who don't have the required competencies, yet show the desired behavioral/emotional attributes.

BEHAVIORAL EXPECTATIONS

Every position requires a specific set of competencies and behaviors. Organizations outline job requirements as a way of reaching a common vision for how the position should be carried out and the work should be executed.

It is easy enough to throw labels or list behavior markers to explain what is expected of a specific job. However, it is more difficult to delineate the coherent types of behavior needed to actually succeed in the position.

We developed a behavior profile for positions that defines the ideal behavior expected for performing a job. It looks like a GRI profile, such as the example below, and contains the four factors, except that there is one graph instead of three. It is analyzed the same way as a GRI profile. We call it the Position Behavior Indicator or PBI.

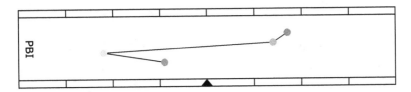

The behavioral/emotional component of a position takes more importance as soon as we can make a nuanced assessment of it. Still, other characteristics are also important. As we saw in our discussion of the talent patchwork in Chapter 3, the behavioral/emotional is simply one component of an individual's talent and what might make them successful in a particular position. Other characteristics such as experience, certificates, skills, and interests, depending on the context, can be integral to a position.

DETERMINING THE MOST FREQUENT BEHAVIORS IN A POSITION

Although positions require individuals to perform different tasks based on a variety of behaviors, we consider here simply the behaviors that need to be most frequently executed. For example, the expected behavior for accountants and salespeople are often different:

- Accountants may need to be attentive to details, patient, and have a deep knowledge of accounting. They are naturally involved with data and in solving complex problems in their field of expertise. They are not expected to make public appearances or display a superficial knowledge of their subject matter.

- Sales representatives may need to be outgoing, know about the products they sell, with enough product knowledge to close deals. But they do not need an in-depth expertise as much as the technicians who make the products or provide support. Their ability to informally connect with anyone helps them reach decision-makers efficiently.

Different techniques can be used to define the ideal profile for a position. We present three of them here:

- A comparison with typical profiles in the industry
- An analysis of the employees currently in the job
- A survey that assesses the most frequent behaviors in the position

Industry Standards

The first option for defining a position is making use of typical profiles, which aggregate the behaviors of people in similar jobs once we have removed any outliers; for example, a typical profile for entrepreneurs, whether they're in Silicon Valley or elsewhere.

"Typical" means that about 60 percent of the natural profiles of entrepreneurs have a similar profile according to our statistics. When considering how entrepreneurs adapt to their role and how their adaptation gets expressed in their Effective profile, the percentage of typical profiles reaches 75 percent.

The 25 percent of remaining entrepreneurs, though they don't match this profile, are successful in their own way too. Among other attributes that make them successful, they are careful to surround themselves with a diverse set of profiles so that their team will supply what the organization needs. They recruit and manage for these differences.

In other situations we see similar behavior profiles for the same jobs across industries and cultures. For instance, the typical profiles for payroll specialists, accounting, coaching, outside sales, client service, and maintenance show comparative overlap.

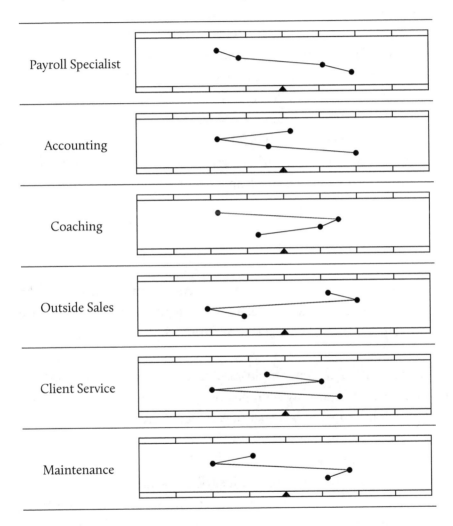

Typical profiles are informative, however, but cannot be used as an all-purpose solution for all companies.

Employees Currently in the Job

Another option is to examine employees who are in the position today. These analyses work best when the organization is satisfied with how current employees are performing. However, there are at least three issues that we need to consider:

1. Only employees who were successfully recruited can be analyzed with this method; the candidates who were filtered out of the organization by not being recruited and who could have eventually been successful, or employees who have already left but would have eventually performed beyond expectations, cannot be accounted for. In other words, you discard characteristics that you are not able to attract or retain in the position.

2. Looking at the profiles does not tell us whether the employees meet their targets and KPIs in the position.

3. It does not account for what will be required in the position in the future. These analyses look at how the past led to what we have today. They do not consider any future changes in the position.

The analysis of current employees, nevertheless, reveals important information about how such positions are being performed today. It highlights adjustments that may be required and can be complemented by an analysis of surveys.

It is important to analyze the profiles of managers because they affect how recruitment and interviews are conducted and how employees in the position are currently being managed. If adjustments are needed, they must come from the managers who are in charge.

SURVEYING JOB NEEDS

The survey is the most easily accessible and simple technique to evaluate a job's requirements. Our survey for defining a position is comprised of twenty-four behavioral propositions that may or may not apply to the job in question. For example, we ask whether the position requires someone to:

1. Lead new plans and initiatives decisively and with authority
2. Follow procedures and comply with standards or rules
3. Accept others' authority with diplomacy and tact

Each proposition needs to be evaluated on a five-point scale depending on how frequently it applies to the position: never, rarely, some of the time, most of the time, or always.

Any survey of this kind should be taken by executives, line managers, recruiting managers, or consultants who have a sound understanding of how the job should be performed.

Is there a right or a wrong perception? Most of the people on a team may have a similar view of the behaviors needed in a position, but one team member's ideas could differ greatly from the rest of the group's. A discussion may need to take place in order to reach a consensus. Each proposition can be discussed individually.

For example, one of the twenty-four propositions, "lead new plans and initiatives decisively and with authority," may be rated as never applying in this role by one participant, whereas one person may reply that it rarely applies, and another that it applies most of the time. The process of creating such a detailed profile forces participants and hiring managers to deal with these different ideas about what a position requires in advance, rather than leaving them open for debate later in the hiring process when candidates have already been interviewed.

This analysis would typically be run in conjunction with the analysis of employees who are already in the position in order to identify whether there is a gap between what is needed for the future and the behaviors that are currently expected. How to fill the gap by recruiting and managing differently in the future should be discussed.

THE ADVANTAGES OF CREATING A POSITION PROFILE

Having a more accurate accounting of the behaviors required for a position can assist with selecting and interviewing job candidates as well as with conducting performance reviews. In recruitment, when the number of individuals applying for a position is large, going through the exercise of evaluating and defining a position can pre-select those who are the closest fit in the same way that other, more common characteristics such as diplomas, resumes, and skills are considered. This may give organizations the opportunity to consider qualified candidates who do not match more traditional characteristics.

> In the case of EMOVA Group, the world's leading retail flower-distribution company, Pascale Wolgensinger, who leads the recruitment of franchisees, wanted to determine which candidates would be the best fit for franchise operators.
>
> "It was a question of who would be best oriented toward a franchise operator's profile, someone who is in the store and who manages the store, who permanently operates it," Pascale explained, "as opposed to those franchisees who have more of what we would call a developer's profile, those who are there at the beginning, and then, somewhere along the

line, that can begin to bore them, so they need to duplicate other points of sale."

To define these two positions, Pascale deployed the GRI survey to EMOVA's existing network of franchisees. What she found is that both operators and developers could be successful at managing floral franchises; however, because developers are more likely to get bored with the routine, they need more opportunities to manage others, drive sales, and expand the business. In this way, Pascale was able to identify ways to effectively support different kinds of franchisees in the EMOVA network.

When the number of candidates is small, the PBI opens up the opportunity to look at candidates differently, bringing to light skills or competencies that are not yet fully developed. Using a profile to assess the behavioral requirements of a specific job empowers organizations to interview and onboard candidates more efficiently.

Luke Brawn, CEO of an industrial construction company, used the PBI to define the profile for the estimating manager he needed to hire. Although he interviewed several candidates for the position who were experienced and had strong resumes, he ultimately decided to promote someone from within whose profile was a better match for the position as they had redefined it, even though she was younger and had less practical experience. "She's got the right personality to lead people, and people were shocked when I put her in charge of that department," Luke said. "Now they're all sitting there saying, 'That was a home run.' That's probably my biggest success story."

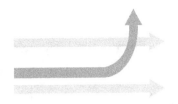

Chapter 15

BUILD TEAMS MORE EFFECTIVELY

Understanding and predicting how one person performs is a challenging task. Understanding and predicting how several people perform together is even more challenging. The number of variables that potentially affect a team's dynamic is obviously more numerous than it is for a single person. Every member of a team affects the behavior of the other members. The type of industry the team is in, the other teams they compete with, informal connections within the organization, and more, all affect the team and its members.

Special challenges may need to be embraced by the team, like developing more innovative ideas, adopting new processes, reorganizing reporting structures, or merging with another team. There is always something happening, whether it's a member entering or leaving, signing a new contract that generates an overload of work, or eventually a lack of work when a contract ends.

Predicting and managing the behavior of the whole may then become an impossible task. But by acknowledging how each member performs distinctly, two by two and all together, we can respond with more creative and effective solutions.

Working on teams and in organizations is where the GRI's journey truly began. Based on my own experiences of growing a team and company, I know that the challenge of managing people quickly shifts from a one-on-one individual focus to the interactions between people and how they function as a group.

Operating in competitive markets forces a company to constantly be more efficient with its people and get better and faster at recruiting, mentoring, making quality decisions, delegating, and alleviating tensions when they occur. In all these tasks, having a better knowledge of how a team functions informs what needs to be done at the individual job level.

Managers may not have to solve clinical cases, but they nevertheless need to have a basic knowledge of psychology—mainly positive psychology—in order to efficiently manage interpersonal dynamics on their own. A better awareness of how individual behavior impacts the team and informs recruitment, promotions, and decisions about change helps managers in situations when they have no one to assist them.

INDIVIDUAL BEHAVIOR AFFECTS TEAMWORK

Working as a team gives us the chance to collaborate with team members who have different skills, abilities, and preferences.

Technology start-ups, consulting practices, government agencies, and nonprofits are all organizations that display distinct overall behaviors that serve specific objectives. This diversity is reflected in the qualities of the employees they hire, reward, and promote as representatives of their company culture. Individuals are attracted to work in organizations where they perceive a fit with their natural way of growing and expressing themselves.

> The more an organization understands the behavioral components required for roles at the job and team levels, and the more those roles complement each other in harmony, the more successful the team will be.

In all of these situations, people's behaviors are at play in groups. Determining the optimal behavior at the team level requires the same precision it does at the individual and position levels.

We can describe the behavior of groups using the same markers we use to describe people and positions. The words can be combined in similar dimensions, enabling analyses of the behavioral aspects at four different levels: individual, position, team, and organization.

THE ORGANIZATION'S TALENT PATCHWORK

The talent patchwork that we saw in Chapter 3 can be used at a team level, similar to the way we use it at individual and position levels. Every company has an overall talent patchwork depending on its industry, history, and culture.

For example, soft characteristics like the core values of a company, its vision, and mission are all distinct at team and organizational levels in order to focus the attention of employees on specific goals and behaviors. These defining characteristics are typically discussed intensely and openly throughout the company. We sometimes see values or mission statements plastered on business cards and bulletin boards. These core concepts are broad and abstract at the organizational level.

How do the behavior profiles, as measured by the GRI, then work with regard to these concepts? In two ways:

1. A person's behavior profile can be compared with the expected behaviors of a position or with the profile of a team. At this level, the profile portrays the overall behavior required from a group.

2. An individual's GRI behavior profile informs us about how that person embraces, expresses, shares, and communicates these core concepts. For instance, very High 1s will push hard with their opinions. Extremely Low 3s and Low 4s will be impetuous. The full profile that maps out the four factors and the three graphs provides an even more refined reading.

In the next section, we discuss how the behavior expected in teams can be used in parallel to analyze teams and organizations.

BEHAVIORAL EXPECTATIONS FOR TEAMS

Fast-growing start-ups targeting an IPO need to behave differently than a government agency such as the DMV. Individuals in different kinds of organizations need to perform and be motivated in different ways.

The overall behavior that companies, divisions, and teams are expected to perform can be modeled similarly to the behaviors required for specific positions. This overall behavior may become an enduring component and part of the organization's DNA and culture.

The Team Behavior Indicator or TBI is the profile that mirrors these behaviors at a group level. It reads like a behavior profile for a position (PBI) or a GRI behavior profile for an individual, with four points and three lines, like the one below.

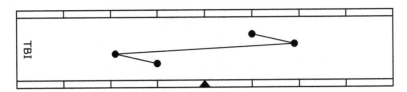

The behavior profile of a team reflects the overall behaviors that an organization needs to display in order to be effective. Behavior profiles for teams are created for specific departments and teams; however, the team profiles at lower levels, the behavior profiles for specific positions, and the behavior profiles of employees must all be coherent with the organization's overall behavior profile.

In a large, uniform team, the behavior profile of a team sets the trend for the dominant position of the team and of the managers who need to align with this trend.

There may, however, be other behavior profiles on the team. For instance, in the example below, the behavior profile is set for a sales team. It mirrors the profiles of the sales representatives who are dominant in this team. However, the team's administrative support and client service positions will be different. The shapes of the profiles reflect those differences.

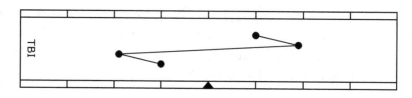

TBI Sales Team

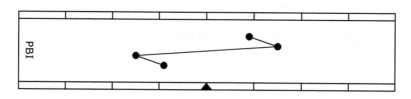

PBI Sales Representative (same as TBI—50 percent)

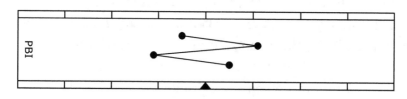

PBI—Client Service (30 percent)

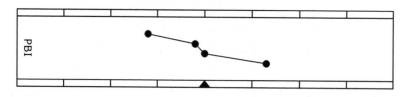

PBI—Sales Admin. (20 percent)

WHY INTEGRATED DIVERSITY IS VALUABLE

Everyone knows that having a baseball team with all catchers on the roster won't win games.

Working as a team gives us the chance to distribute tasks among team members based on their diverse competencies, skills, abilities, experiences, and interests, as well as their distinct way of performing. When the work is balanced across a diverse team, there are more diverse viewpoints, competencies, and ways of self-expression that complement rather than compete with each other.

Combining the strengths of two or more different profiles will eventually result in an advantage that is greater than their sum. In this way, you can avoid too much overlap and develop a positive appreciation of the differences between employees.

The reverse situation is a uniform team where all members share the same background, characteristics, experiences, diplomas, and more. When we analyze large teams of people who have the same responsibilities—for instance, sales, client service, consulting, legal, or accounting—regardless of their diploma, age, gender, or culture, some typical patterns and commonalities emerge. This happens because their jobs have similar aspects and demands, including behavioral/emotional requirements.

Uniform teams face different challenges than diverse teams, the nature of which depend on the common characteristics shared by the team and what may be lacking from time to time.

In either case, whether a team is diverse or uniform, its members should be aware of what is expected of each of them as team members, and continuously and efficiently adjust their style and communication.

OPTIMIZE COLLABORATION

Since so much information about team members has to be processed in real time, data that is condensed, visual, memorable, and instantly actionable is a more effective guide to recalibrating teams than using intuitive impressions.

Personal data reveals much information about a person's behavior, motivation, adaptation, and engagement within a specific work environment. Obviously, disengagement and negative emotions are counterproductive for team members. Minimizing these elements by taking into account how each team member behaves and is motivated can save an organization significant time, money, and frustration.

An individual's profile can be compared with the profiles of other team members, the expected behavior for the position, and with the overall behavior expected of the team.

By recognizing the nature of the work to be accomplished by the team, how the team needs to perform as a whole, and the requirements of each position, each member can be more effectively understood and engaged in productive behaviors.

Analyzing the GRI behavior profiles of the team individually, then by pairs of people, and then finally all together as a team, provides us with new insights and more effective solutions for managing a team of people. The following examples demonstrate this.

Individual Conversations

Working on improving a team's performance typically starts with all team members taking the GRI survey and gaining a better self-awareness of their own talents, strengths, and motivations.

Individual improvements and teamwork improvements accompany this process.

Once the team's behavior profiles are understood and validated at the individual level, it's easier to share them among the entire team. The GRI platform supports this experience by providing access to the results online and tools to organize conversations about the feedback in person or via the Internet.

Receiving feedback from a certified GRI user, who either sits within your company or is external, is an important step in the process of learning the behavior profile's benefits and answering questions about the system. The feedback or conversations, however, quickly involve aspects related to a specific job and teammates who need to be addressed directly, either between two people or at the team level.

Analyzing Two People

When considering two people, let's say Dennis and Catherine, displaying their two behavior profiles side by side helps us discern how they interact and work together. What it takes for Dennis to match Catherine's style is revealed in their Natural profiles, factor by factor. The more distant each of Dennis's factors is from Catherine's, the more effort it takes to match styles.

The rule of thumb for considering how people get along (or not) despite their differences is to look at how distant the profiles are from each other. The percentage of similarity produced by the platform is an indicator of that distance. 100 percent similarity means that the two profiles are identical. Zero percent similarity reveals profiles that are far distant from each other.

In the following example, Dennis and Catherine have similar Natural profiles (82 percent similar). The small vectors displayed show the extent to which each factor would have to change in one profile in order to match the other person's profile. With similar profiles, the two individuals work in comparable ways.

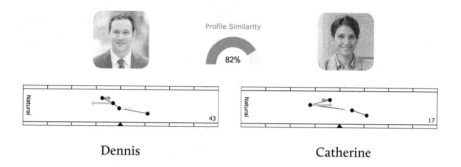

Dennis   Catherine

UNDERSTANDING TEAM DYNAMICS

Viewing the behavior profiles side by side, as in the above example, works well with two people. When the number of profiles grows, displaying them in relation to the team's leader with the help of the GRI platform instantly puts important characteristics in perspective and raises questions about how the different members influence each other.

The most salient characteristics of the profiles show up first, along with questions about how these characteristics impact the team. The comparisons we performed above two by two can also be done here, except that there are more combinations.

If we see that the members are not engaged, that raises questions about the potential reasons for the lack of engagement: Is it coming from the team environment, the personal environment of each member, or from within the team? How does the communication style of the manager affect the team?

Considering the adaptation efforts at the team level raises additional questions about how the team perceives the need to change: How well does the adaptation effort of each person match what is expected of the team?

As a result of harnessing the power of the GRI to analyze team dynamics, Mary Lou Song, executive chairman of FuelX, found that "Sharing survey results with each of our team members has been enlightening. The GRI helps them understand themselves and also other team members. It also helps us identify and articulate what we value in our team and how we want to grow our company."

Other graphic illustrations may be more appropriate when, as in sports, the physical location on the field or in a boat for rowing or sailing is important to the position. For example, in rowing, the position of the coxswain has a distinct importance. Each rower's seat corresponds to a different position on the team. Analysis of the team makes more sense when the profiles are displayed in relation to each other, as in the diagram below.

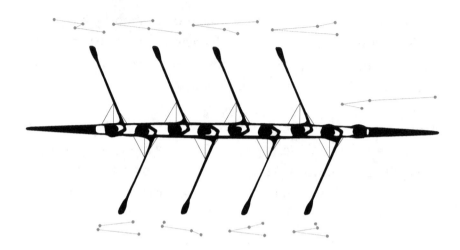

For analyzing teams of various sizes, the GRI platform presents the data through scatter charts, tables, grids, and other powerful diagrams to instantly reveal the team's diversity, behaviors that may be missing, or how the team aligns with the overall targeted behaviors required.

Sharing Profiles within the Team

For a broader understanding of behaviors, a 2 x 2 grid enables us to grasp the interpersonal dynamics on a team. We call this grid the standard grid and the four groups in it the primary groups. The four groups are determined by the factor that's the highest in the GRI profile. For instance, Group 1 regroups all profiles where Factor 1 is the highest.

People will get along more easily with those in the quadrants adjacent to them on either side. For example, those in Group 1 will get along best with people in Group 2 and Group 4.

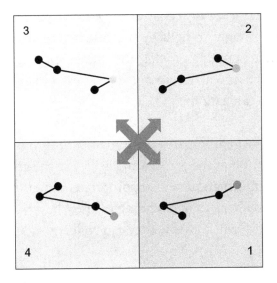

Team Dynamics

People who fall into the mirrored profiles, the ones facing diagonally across the center of the grid, have the most potential differences to deal with. In situations of conflict, people with the most divergent profiles will tend to criticize each other the most. For instance, people in Group 1 will naturally reproach those in Group 3 for not taking the initiative and being too consensual, too slow, and too risk averse.

How team members and their behavior profiles show up in these four groups reveals the frictions that may typically emerge between them, and what needs to be done to avoid and resolve these frictions in advance.

Providing team members with access to the standard grid so that they may view the connections between their individual results with other profiles two by two, as we saw above with Dennis and Catherine, facilitates their recognition of the dynamics within the team.

As is often the case with matters regarding people, sharing the information brought to light by the GRI in a team requires sensitivity, an understanding of what the information is about, and an advanced GRI user who can monitor progress, either from inside or outside the organization.

The GRI platform automates team member regrouping and eases the interpretation of the profiles and access to the grid. Ultimately, sharing the information with appropriate monitoring improves each team member's understanding of their best way to perform, how others perform, and how they can collectively succeed.

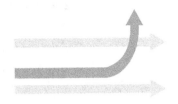

Chapter 16

DESIGN ORGANIZATIONS THAT THRIVE

Making sense of how an organization functions, whether it's a small team, a large company, or one of its divisions, requires considering all of its constituents, its people—most often starting with those who occupy leadership positions—and their characteristics. In doing so, a handful of the most salient characteristics typically emerge. Sometimes we point out a team member's past experience in a similar job, the skills they have developed, or the diploma they earned at a top school. In other situations, we may be more focused on the quality of the relationships people have grown or how they met their sales targets. In any case, these behavioral/ emotional characteristics can be assessed subjectively through intuitive responses, like "He's a good guy" and "She stays late every day," or more objectively with tools like the GRI.

As the organization grows, it becomes more difficult for senior management to assess all the behavioral/emotional characteristics of new team members since recruitment and management has been delegated further down the organization to managers and HR professionals. Yet senior management at the top of the organization has the overall vision for what the organization aims to accomplish and knows best the kinds of characteristics needed to be successful in this pursuit. Thus, how behavioral/emotional characteristics are managed at all levels becomes more and more diluted and challenging the faster and bigger a company scales.

From an organizational and managerial standpoint, a performance-driven company requires individual and group behaviors that can procure a competitive advantage and that typically cover a broad spectrum. Teams and organizations display different overall behaviors depending on their expertise, industry, and maturity. The larger the organization, the more types of behaviors that are distributed among distinct teams.

By reviewing an organization from the top down to all its employees in all departments, teams, and levels, the opportunities to improve a company's recruitment, management, and development become evident. Most personality assessments provide information on individuals that is objective, reliable, and relevant to the workplace, but they do little to solve the organizational challenges of hiring and managing people and implementing change from the top.

Working with small and large organizations in different industries and cultures over the years has given us further opportunities to gather knowledge and create unique tools that utilize personality measurements at a group level and can scale up to be used in companies.

The GRI cloud platform helps to analyze individual profiles within teams and the larger company, and can be used for recruitment. When deployed as an enterprise solution, it assists in regrouping individual profiles with a few clicks so that analyses can be run effortlessly. Data and maps based on the profile results, like the examples in this book, can be instantly produced by the platform.

ANALYZING LARGE GROUPS

One of the main reasons for analyzing large groups and regrouping profiles is to gain a broad awareness of the tendencies of the group members, which extends to various subjects, including how team members generally express their leadership and creativity and how they communicate, delegate, manage, make decisions, and learn.

This in turn provides an understanding of what the members of the group need, and how they would like to be rewarded, motivated, and supported in the organization. By reviewing the profiles once they have been regrouped into categories, we can generate maps and indicators that can be compared with the expectations of leaders and managers for their organization.

When analyzing large groups, let's say groups of 100, 1,000, or 200,000 people, putting profiles side by side does not work anymore, so it is necessary to regroup them into categories. This is done by considering the different shapes of the individual behavior profiles that make up the team.

We saw in the preceding chapter that the first step to mapping a large number of profiles is to make use of a 2 x 2 grid where the profiles are regrouped according to the highest factor in the group, which we call the standard grid. For a more refined analysis, we use the 6 x 4 grid below called the refined grid. The twenty-four profiles in it are all possible arrangements of the four GRI factors.

As with the behavior profiles for individuals, we refer to the grids as we would a road map, only they map out a group of people instead of a territory. Just as a road map is a big picture that helps us navigate the land and avoid getting lost, the grid guides us to navigate the complex reality of how a large number of people perform together.

The platform provides other maps for analyzing people who are in the same team, sub-teams, and positions. These grids and profiles provide answers—most often instantly and visually, thanks to the maps and shapes of the profiles—to questions such as:

- Which teams display higher levels of engagement?
- What are the most represented reference profiles?
- How much do team members adapt to their positions?
- How uniform or distant are the behaviors of the people being compared to each other?
- Who are the outliers and how do they differ from the rest of the group?

Group analyses sometimes call for adjusting communication and managerial style; in other situations, they call for shifting the way new candidates are recruited, interviewed, and onboarded. Making changes at the organizational level based on these results usually requires the involvement of leaders. Decisions can be made and executed from the top based on how people at your organization deal with change, which is informed by the behavior profiles.

> As Marcus Clarke-Gross, principal at accounting firm REDW, said: "Once everyone had taken the assessment, the value of the GRI distribution chart was a real eye-opener. Finally, I could see what I suspected about how our team worked together. Understanding adaptation in GRI was the best thing I did for the well-being of my individual staff and managers. I clearly saw the effort each made every day to be what he or she thought we wanted, often unnecessarily. Unbelievable!"

When group analyses are conducted during trainings, they instantly convey the decisions and actions that need to be taken by participants. For instance, strong adaptation and disengagement may be revealed in the team, or adjustments in a few jobs may need to be made immediately.

> New measurements reveal information that was not available before; if needed, they may even call for changes to be made.

In the following sections, we briefly explain how group-level analyses work in some situations of organizational development and sales, and how these analyses further inform executive decisions and actions.

THE EVOLUTION OF AN ORGANIZATION

We can analyze and manage how an organization's behavior profile evolves over time by using the standard grid. The behavior of an organization typically follows this cycle: Group 1 marks the start-up phase, Group 2 and Group 3 are characterized by rapid growth and building a loyal customer base, and Group 4 leads to strengthening the organization's processes, as illustrated below. Once an organization makes it to Group 4, that usually signals a need to restart through innovative projects and move back to Group 1.

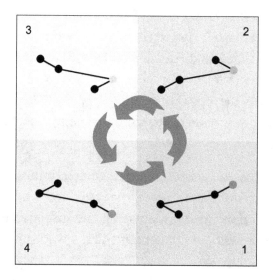

Evolution Over Time

To discover which stage of the cycle your organization is in requires first obtaining all of the individual behavior profiles within the organization. Once these are obtained, the GRI platform automatically maps them in the standard grid according to the position and team they are in.

Jumping from Group 4 of the evolution cycle described above, where organizations are well established and set in their ways, back to

Group 1, where organizations operate like start-ups and take bigger risks, is a difficult transition.

In order to be more like Group 1 organizations, you'll need to recruit people who have Group 1 profiles; yet their behavioral preferences make them a mismatch to work at a Group 4 organization. The emotional labor required to adapt to the behavior profile of Group 4 will quickly push those people out.

How, then, to proceed when a reboot is needed? Provide those whose profiles fall into Group 1 with what they need: independence, challenges, fast-paced decision-making, and the absence of strict oversight. It's not easy for organizations in Group 4 to do this since they often have many processes and rules in place. However, it can be accomplished by creating independent project units or incubators that exist within the company or by financing outside ventures.

APPLYING GRID ANALYSIS

The grid analysis and method can be used to rejuvenate and reform specific departments or teams within your organization, such as a sales force. In sales, there are generally two strategies or schools of thought. The first strategy views salespeople as farmers: they close sales with existing clients or clients that spontaneously seek their product or services based on word-of-mouth referrals and marketing efforts, rather than actively reaching out to clients to stimulate business. Salespeople who operate according to this style correspond to the behaviors typically identified in Group 3 and Group 4.

The second school of thought views salespeople as hunters and embraces a strategy that is the opposite of the farmers'. Hunters reach out to prospective clients and experience frequent rejections, rather than waiting for clients to approach them. This behavior is typically what we find in Group 1 and Group 2.

Analyzing the sales force with the standard grid gives a clear and immediate comprehension of the team's behavior and how they typically engage with clients to close sales, whether they're naturally farmers or hunters.

How marketing efforts help the sales force close client deals also needs to be analyzed. The behavior profile of the sales force as a group reveals whether the hunter or farmer style of behavior can be realistically enforced onto each sales representative, and at what level of intensity. Again, any adaptation from one style to the other will generate emotional labor for individuals who behave more naturally one way than another, and that can translate into disengagement and a failure to deliver results further down the line.

Discovering what needs to change in order for the sales force to drive more results starts with an analysis of the profiles that are in place today, what is needed to realistically motivate and engage them more—information provided by individual GRI profiles—and how marketing is involved in the process.

A change in strategy, whether it calls for salespeople to switch from a farmer to hunter, or vice versa, also requires change in the recruitment process and management approach. Enforcing one style over the other will generate disengagement and, consequently, underperformance and employee turnover.

DEFINING YOUR ORGANIZATION'S CORE BEHAVIORS

A company's unique competitive edge in the market and ability to generate long-term returns on investment is a function of how the organization communicates, stimulates creativity, re-engineers its processes, and merges with or acquires other organizations. How these various events and scenarios unfold is critical for an organization's success.

By identifying an organization's aggregate profile, the GRI indicates how it will change, make decisions, develop trust, and encourage creativity and radical innovation.

At Owens Design, a company based in Silicon Valley that manufactures custom, high-tech equipment, CEO John Apgar used the GRI to discover the core characteristics that define their company culture and workforce. "We have a strong concentration of profiles here and what we found is that really everyone in the organization is either highly dominant or highly analytical," John said. "There really is no one in the organization that would be considered a patient person or a highly social person. That's, I think, important as we continue to recruit people into the company that we understand what that concentration is and, frankly, if someone is a very patient person, they tend not to enjoy the culture here."

Specialized services such as accounting, legal, executive search, executive coaching, or software development, to name a few, all have different behavior profiles as a group. For the sake of performance and efficiency, services like these may be contracted outside the organization; the behavior profiles of freelancers or independent contractors may be better matched for certain kinds of tasks and more easily hired and managed at a lesser cost outside the organization.

The services that an organization wants to keep in house depend on its capacity to manage them effectively; the greater the difference between the behavior profiles for these services and those at the core of the organization, the greater the effort required to manage and motivate the individuals who offer those services. As a general rule, GRI behavior profiles need to be in sync with what is required by specific jobs and the organization as a whole.

SHIFTING ORGANIZATIONAL BEHAVIORS OVER TIME

An organization's behavior can be transformed and channeled toward the desired result expressed in the profiles for the positions and teams:

- Pay attention to the behavior profiles of individuals who more closely match the behaviors expected in the position during recruitment. With time, company growth, and the natural turnover of employees, team members who have a Natural profile closer to the desired behavior profiles for the position will be more numerous in the overall organization.

- Manage team members in a thoughtful way that reflects their intrinsic motivations and the demands of their job as they were designed in the positions. Provide them with the attention needed for building trusted relationships and an efficient dynamic within the team. These efforts will be reflected in the Role profiles, which should match the behaviors expected in the position.

- Ensure that, as a consequence of more appropriate recruitment and management actions, the behaviors displayed by team members progressively match the expected behaviors expressed in the jobs, teams, and overall organization. The Effective profiles should, in time, better match the behaviors at job and team levels as defined by management.

As the data continues to be gathered, analyzed, and shared, your organization must be able to display more coherence over time with what is expected from it.

> Natalie Kennedy, the director of operations and compliance at Stanford Investment Group, took advantage of the GRI's insights not only to better define the kind of individual who thrives at their company, but also to shift their service model to more of a team approach. "We really felt the GRI knowledge of individuals revealed their natural selves and allowed us to put them on teams and formulate how they would be able to work together, which worked very well," Natalie explained. It helped us identify why two personalities couldn't get along because they communicated in a different manner, or why some individuals work extremely well together because they have similar traits."

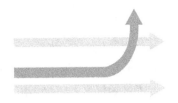

Chapter 17

FORGET EVERYTHING YOU THOUGHT YOU KNEW ABOUT PEOPLE

Learning new systems to assess personality may excite some and worry others. Reactions were the same when the first airplanes took flight and the first cars took to the road. Pilots and drivers alike had to prove they could reach their destination.

Personality assessments have been around for more than a century now. As in the early days of aviation, some people have had an unlucky, crash-and-burn experience with assessments. Today we are well acquainted with the limitations of these tools.

An important aspect of personality measurements is their soft and reflexive nature. The thing being assessed—personality—looks subjective and fuzzy. Because of this, the journey to realize the potential benefits of personality assessments always starts with ourselves: What does this assessment say about me that I don't know yet and may agree with? What is the value for me? The journey continues incrementally and concomitantly in practice with real subjects.

Over the years, we have found that the process of learning the GRI behavior profiles is a transformational experience that is valuable for fostering leadership capabilities. Tapping into objective information and effective strategies for managing people is central in developing soft skills.

Just as with optical instruments, the GRI assessment extends our vision to discern nuances that we could not see before. It offers us new representations via the profiles that help us solve important questions related to ourselves, our colleagues, and our organization.

The learning process occurs in three steps, as if we were looking through three different lenses. First, we look at the GRI behavior profiles, our own and others, which is like looking at the world with a magnifying glass. Then, as if we are raising a periscope, we look over our heads to see what is required in our position and how those expectations affect us. Finally, we use a telescope to look further away at our organization and its place in the market.

KNOW THYSELF AND OTHERS

The first step of learning the GRI behavior profiles requires us to look at our own characteristics. Doing this helps us to better distinguish our best way to perform and others'; it also encourages us to be motivated and engaged.

The talent patchwork, the four factors, and the GRI profile allow us to look at ourselves and others with new eyes. We begin to see nuances that prompt us to ask new questions, consider potential challenges differently, and find more creative and effective answers and solutions.

SET REALISTIC EXPECTATIONS

Learning about the behaviors expected in various positions in an organization invites us to consider the job demands that we and other people in the organization may experience. It helps build an understanding of how people are required to perform, not in the abstract, but by adjusting to the demands of their job in real time.

People are motivated, engaged, and energized in their work in different ways. The GRI provides clues for how to motivate and engage specific profiles, and gives organizations, its leaders, managers, and HR experts the power to envision creative solutions for the future.

EXTEND THE GRI'S REACH TO THE TEAM AND ORGANIZATIONAL LEVELS

After developing a new appreciation of how people work and relate to their jobs, the next step of learning is expanding your knowledge of how people relate to each other and how they function within their team and organization.

As we saw previously, the GRI platform helps to display, aggregate, and analyze the profiles of teams and larger numbers of people. Examining profiles in this way provides an instant comparison of how individuals respond to the demands of their jobs and teams.

This third part of the training offers a more refined picture of how the whole organization functions, and how the organization's profile reflects all of its positions and the people who occupy them.

LEARN AND PRACTICE SIMULTANEOUSLY

From our experience training executives, managers, and people experts in the GRI through a variety of methods—the Internet, blended approaches, with textbooks—we've realized that nothing works as effectively as social interaction in a three-day training format. We call it the GRI seminar.

One key aspect of learning and applying the GRI is that it takes a lot of energy to reshape our thinking about how we believe human beings behave and are motivated. This cannot be stressed enough.

Part of the reason, as we saw in Chapter 2, is that the GRI challenges sensitive, built-in knowledge we have about ourselves and others, something that is fundamental to us as humans. This is not knowledge one reconsiders or changes lightly. It takes some effort and a mandate to retrain the way you think about people. What we learn from the GRI likely forces us to reconsider what we already know about people, in particular, those closest to us whom we believe we know so well.

Learning the behavior profiles requires taking the survey, experiencing the results, sharing the results, asking questions, receiving answers, and so on to continue the learning process, regardless of our education or responsibility level in the org chart. Learning about the behavior profiles is very much like acquiring a new language: it requires practice, reading, and speaking it out loud with real people and real organizations.

Using the GRI as a language, we learn and practice simultaneously how to improve people-related matters. This process is accelerated by facilitation from a GRI expert and social interaction with the other participants, as well as through the tools provided by the GRI platform.

Literacy in the GRI is pivotal for capturing the value of the system's numerous applications. Working on the issues at hand in an organization while learning the GRI helps uncover hidden issues from within and fix them immediately. Team members benefit from the seminar training which helps them be better understood by their colleagues, and at the same time, become capable of better understanding other team members and managers.

"The seminar experience for learning about the GRI was very intensive," said Natalie Kennedy of the Stanford Investment Group. "It's a three-day seminar, so you have a little understanding about the GRI when you go in, but when you come in you learn all the parameters on day one. The second day was great because you're taking that knowledge and then actually talking through presenting it to somebody...once you get comfortable speaking about it, it becomes very easy."

The GRI platform plays a central role in deploying the GRI at organizations. It distributes surveys to remote locations on a global scale, aggregates and analyzes results, and provides resources for continued study of the behavior profiles. GRI experts facilitate this process and are available to answer questions and maximize the benefits of the GRI at an organization.

OLD HABITS ARE HARD TO BREAK

A trusted relationship can form instantly and effortlessly in the first minutes of two people meeting. Trust may also dissolve suddenly and unexpectedly, making a relationship tense and difficult. That's because trust and confidence are informed by our intuition and instinctive reactions to people.

There is now an increasing awareness that our perceptions and judgments are affected by many biases, such as stereotyping and selective perception, as we discussed in Chapter 1.

As we saw in Part I, data about the behavior profiles does not come from our intuition. It is produced from people's answers to the GRI survey. The results invite us to adjust our understanding of people and make decisions that better match a person's natural proclivities and the demands of their job, rather than our first impressions.

We can accelerate the process of training by building trust through the benefits of the GRI profiles. As indicated above, this comes with experiencing the profiles of real people in practical situations, with facilitation and support.

Holding our first impressions of people and refraining from making unnecessary inferences or judging too fast is what successful managers naturally do. They quickly perceive the value of the behavior profiles to assist in the understanding, adjustment, and decision-making about people. This process may take many years or decades, but the GRI can greatly accelerate it.

> Mary Lou Song of FuelX recalled: "My brother and I cofounded a company. We assumed we knew how best to work together. The seminar made us realize how powerful the GRI is in helping people build teams. Now we're not just siblings; we're strong business partners."

Learning about and implementing the GRI is a transformative experience for people and organizations.

"When I completed the seminar, it was within a day or two that I realized that it was pivotal in my understanding," commented one executive at a client company in Palo Alto who attended the seminar. "As a result, two things: One, I was able to address whoever it was I was working with in a different way that helped things to be more effective, removed friction from the relationship, things that get in the way that cause hiccups; The second part was that I had a better understanding of myself and what that fundamental wiring was and what it actually means to choose what I do and how I show up."

TEACH A PERSON TO FISH

We train executives, managers, and people experts alike to take advantage of the GRI system's many possible applications. As explained above, the GRI seminar combines acquiring new knowledge and then applying it in real situations. The seminar experience is as much training as it is consulting. The result is a transformative experience for participants that is immediately applicable to their own workplace.

The information provided by the GRI is meant to be used immediately and by the people who need it the most: the individual who has taken the GRI survey, the manager who wants to monitor and improve the performance of their team members, the recruiter who needs to interview and recommend candidates, and the executives running the organization at its highest levels.

Executives and managers, as well as recruiters, people specialists, executive coaches, and leadership and organizational development experts can all become experts at using the GRI through training.

The GRI's performance-driven system invites leaders to make decisions about people using methodologies devoid of bias, proactively work toward diversity and inclusion goals, engage team members, and develop leaders for superior performance. These are critical issues facing every business in operation today.

While executives and managers are not typically involved in the day-to-day implementation of the GRI, teaching them to speak the same language and become as knowledgeable in the GRI as their people experts dramatically impacts the benefits the GRI delivers to them, their team, and their entire organization. They use it to make better-informed decisions about people in situations where they are on their own, on the spot, and frequently so, such as communicating during meetings, interviewing and onboarding candidates, or solving conflicts when they suddenly arise.

GRI experts and advanced certified users accompany its deployment, assisting with feedback, interviewing, or guiding further actions with the GRI. Executive coaching and other individual or group services may take advantage of the GRI from inside or outside the organization. The larger the organization, the more the GRI needs orchestration and expert knowledge from the human resources department. However, training and consulting expertise in the GRI naturally comes from outside the organization, beginning with the three-day GRI seminar.

With minimal practice, you gain agility with the behavior profiles and realize its benefits for recruitment, management, and leadership. GRI literacy then opens up avenues for taking people and your organization's performance to a whole new level.

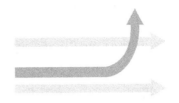

FREQUENTLY ASKED QUESTIONS

Do GRI behavior profiles change?

The short answer is that a person's Natural doesn't generally change that much, but their Role profile may change more often since environments change more often. A more detailed answer is that it depends on different factors. The Natural does not change for most people, but it may for a very few of us, depending on the intensity of each factor and the visibility of the profile (see Chapter 4). If you consider profiles that are retaken after long periods, for example, after five years or more, Natural profiles are most often consistent in shape and intensity with the first survey results.

Can people fake their results?

As with measurement in any field of science, it is possible to fake the results if you really put some effort into it! However, it's hard to do that and very unlikely to happen with the GRI. For the first question in the survey, it's up to you to decide how you want to answer it; there is not much to fake. When we become aware of a situation where someone has tampered with their profile results, we will send a warning. We have internal solutions for dealing with these unlikely cases.

How does the GRI differentiate from other systems?

The GRI survey assesses a limited number of core dimensions of personality, motivation, and adaptation, which altogether form a nuanced understanding of people, although most systems assess a list of traits or types that often overlap, and can be used differently by different people. By combining the visual profiles with performance analytics, the GRI is used seamlessly in a large scope of applications, whereas most systems are restricted to few of them. The GRI brings to executives and managers a more effective way to make decisions and build a performance-driven organization; most systems remain in the hands of few people.

Is the GRI survey reliable and valid for hiring?

Yes, it is. Thorough statistics have been performed to insure validity and reliability and demonstrate that the survey does not have an adverse impact on people of different sexes, ethnic backgrounds, or ages. The GRI was devised for workplace-related applications. It does not measure clinical traits. It assesses dimensions that are already assessed by other techniques in the workplace, including methods like interviews, but it does so more objectively and effectively with a visual language that removes some pervasive biases that may exist in the organization.

How can I deploy the GRI in my company?

The first step to deploying the GRI in your company is becoming knowledgeable about the system and its use, while receiving support and assistance through trainings and GRI consulting associates. The GRI training is the most critical component. The executive retreat and trainings for recruiters and managers are deployed according to your company's current and future needs. We provide services to assist you and your HR professionals with group presentations, executive search and recruitment, team-building workshops, and one-on-one feedback sessions. Our assistance extends to helping employees access their results on the GRI platform and participate in our GRI Discovery program through a series of webinars, which can be provided from either inside your organization by certified users or by our GRI consulting associates.

How does executive coaching work with GRI?

More nuanced and objective information about people can benefit and enhance one-on-one conversations with executive coaches and in group sessions. However, executive coaching does not typically address hiring, the point at which many issues with employees may start. Neither does executive coaching typically become involved in organizational development, where issues may have also started. Some of our GRI experts have successfully coached leaders for decades; some of them have received certification from international coaching associations. They all acknowledge the limits of executive coaching and the benefits of the GRI seminar for removing the pervasive effects of biases. The GRI provides executives and managers with a visual language that can prevent frictions ahead of time and help coaching be more impactful.

How are recruiters involved with the GRI?

In order for recruiters to make use of the GRI during the recruitment process, they need first to attend a GRI training with a focus on what pertains most to recruitment: attracting, selecting, interviewing, and onboarding appropriate candidates. For groups of recruiters in larger organizations, the training can be organized with remote sessions, or in a blended way by combining on-site and remote sessions. We assist with implementing the GRI into the recruitment processes, defining PBIs, and determining when to deliver feedback and conduct interviews.

Do line managers get involved with the GRI?

Line managers use the GRI to develop their leadership, interview and recruit new team members, and improve their team's performance. This starts with attending a GRI training. For larger organizations, the GRI training is organized in a blended way by combining on-site and remote sessions. Along with leadership development professionals at your company, we remain available to assist in the implementation of the GRI in teams and with new candidates.

How do 360-degree surveys work alongside the GRI?

A 360-degree survey informs us on the impressions we have about others and how we see them. In contrast, the GRI profile reveals how someone is influenced by others to change (the Role profile), as well as their intrinsic motivation, which is not informed by a 360-degree survey. There are different types of 360-degree surveys, and those that best complement the GRI suggest how teammates can improve without making personal judgments. The GRI provides incremental information about how our impressions of others are formed and invites us to look at job requirements, too, in order to resolve potential friction or improve performance.

How do engagement surveys work with the GRI?

Engagement surveys exist in different forms, including the recent advent pulse surveys, thanks to the Internet and mobile interfaces. The GRI provides a different assessment of engagement, which we explained in Chapter 4: results from the interaction between individuals and their environment. The Engagement Level measured by the GRI survey does not require assessment on a regular basis as pulse surveys do, but only after key events such as a promotion or a training. Although the information provided by engagement surveys is valuable, as it is with 360-feedback, the GRI provides additional information that helps improve teammates' engagement by revealing their intrinsic motivations. At the same time, the GRI is more objective and nuanced about the needs of the organization.

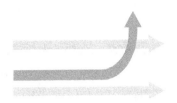

NEXT STEPS

How can I know about what the GRI says about my leadership style?
What is your leadership style? How do you continue to leverage your talents and strengths as a leader and perform at the top of your game? Who else do you need to bring onto your team and in what capacity? The GRI offers more accurate sense of how you can continue to grow.

If you haven't done so already, take the GRI survey now. If your organization has an annual Service and License Agreement (SLA), ask to take the GRI survey as part of the program. If no program is in place, go to our website (**www.gri.co/lead**) and receive a discount when you take the survey within 30 days of purchasing this book. The results will be private. When you take the GRI survey, you will receive your GRI profile and analysis, as well as other options like joining our Discovery program, which allows you to access webinars, share results, and ask a GRI expert questions.

How can we start the GRI at our company?

There are several options for starting the GRI at your company, depending on the nature of the points to address. Here are a few possibilities:

1. Attend the GRI Seminar on your own

This is where your experience starts taking shape for everyday, practical use in your executive role. You can either choose to focus on your individual organization and take a seminar with the top executives from your company, or attend a GRI seminar designed for executives from different companies. The GRI seminar is held off-site in various locations globally and requires a three-day commitment.

2. Bring your executives to a retreat

Invite your executives to discover and experience the GRI's transformational power. With information that's accurate, they will learn about each other, your teams, and the organization as a whole. Engage in strategic discussions to foster a performance-driven culture and more effective hiring, management, and development of your organization with the GRI.

3. Request an executive team presentation

Introduce the GRI to your team at your next executive meeting. Ask everyone to take the GRI survey and then schedule one of our GRI experts to share the results and meet with your team. This will give you a better feel for how the GRI works, what it can do for you and your company in the long term, and how investing in the GRI seminar will help you maximize your return.

4. Visit Our Website: www.gri.co
Explore the best next step for you to take advantage of the GRI:

- Discover our services that assist with recruitment and team building; then attend the GRI seminar.

- Contact us. We will analyze your needs and make the best recommendation for the next step using the GRI.

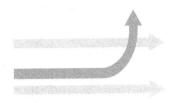

Appendix

FIELDWORK IN PERSONALITY

Research in social sciences and organizations is comparable to exploring faraway lands like Marco Polo sailing to Asia or Captain Cook setting off for Australia from Europe. You are not sure what you will find, but curiosity and an eagerness to set eyes on new sights is what kicks off the adventure and sends you out looking.

As a young CEO, I attempted to adopt more scientific assessment techniques into my leadership, which led me to spend more and more time reading about personality. The personality assessment systems I encountered were inconsistent. I was skeptical about their applicability in everyday business scenarios, but the massive volume of research and recent progress in personality assessment and organizational behavior signaled that future breakthroughs were just around the corner.

It was in this context that I decided to go back to university at the age when many others become CEOs. My career path was turned upside down, but I figured that I could combine the experience I had gained in starting and growing a company with the academic rigor of studying personality. My focus had already pivoted from high-tech to leadership development, and I had ample time and support for conducting academic research. This work later led me to develop the GRI.

RESEARCH IN THE SOCIAL SCIENCES

Field research in the social sciences consists of going out into the field and collecting information through various methods, analyzing and trying to make sense of what you find, and ultimately, answering your primary research question. You propose and consider hypotheses and models, and then eventually test them. This exploration is informed by relevant theories and concepts.

In my case, the field I studied was that of organizations and their actors, which I observed over a period of ten years. Such a large field ensured that the model I was developing would include many perspectives from various executives at different companies.

It sometimes takes more than a year for a researcher to clarify the general question they wish to address. I started with the question: "How do scientifically researched assessment techniques help resolve organizations' challenges?" This was a good starting point, but the question needed to be more specific.

I later refined the question to target how the use of personality assessments by executives would improve an organization's performance. This question opened up analysis of a large range of techniques used in organizations: What do the techniques measure, exactly? How do they compare with each other? Who uses them? Since the research was driven by a focus on performance, it forced me to reconsider our definition of performance and think beyond the limitations of KPIs.

Instead of simply exploring how expert users utilize assessment techniques in organizations, I decided to look at how all potential users make use of these assessments—and since I had the chance to experience the process myself, CEOs and executives were included too.

My sample consisted of 1,100 individuals working at different organizations in various industries and countries on five continents: 214 individuals were CEOs, 317 were executives in C-level positions, 123 individuals were HR directors, and 210 were recruiters or in charge of leadership development. Another category regrouped people who worked outside of companies, including seventy-four executive coaches and consultants, twenty-two university professors, twenty journalists, five lawyers, four researchers in human resources, four angel investors, two medical doctors, and two priests. The remaining hundred or so individuals were employees with no management responsibilities.

The individuals were between the ages of eighteen and eighty. Men and women were equally represented, with more women in HR functions than men. A total of 22 percent were from companies with more than 2,000 employees, 23 percent were from companies with between 300 and 2,000 employees, and 35 percent were from companies with between ten and 300 employees. The remaining 20 percent were self-employed or were from companies with fewer than ten employees.

A large variety of industries were represented in the 500 companies, with 19 percent from the service sector, including hospitality companies and staffing agencies, 9 percent from retail, 7 percent from banking and insurance, 7 percent from publishing, broadcasting, and communication agencies, 4 percent from academia and business schools, 4 percent from nonprofit organizations, and the remaining 37 percent from all other sectors including software, pharmaceutical, legal, accounting, and the military.

More than 1,500 notes were taken over the course of interviewing the 1,100 individuals. I coded these notes using 115 indicators and built a model to track the use of personality assessments, the quality of the assessments, the antecedent variables, the users, and the resulting impact. The fieldwork and construction of the model followed the norms established in social science and qualitative research, notably those defined by Matthew Miles, Michael Huberman, and Kathleen Eisenhardt.

I initially analyzed sixty-eight personality assessments. The model I put into place allowed me to compare and contrast other assessment techniques, including more personal and intimate forms of assessment. The other techniques I formally researched and analyzed include the following: structured interviews, group interviews, 360-degree feedback, reference checks, assessment centers, resumes, biodata, and work samples.

The model I built was developed to bring new insights to various assessment techniques: What did the assessments measure? How were they used and by whom? How were they deployed in organizations? How did these assessment techniques compete and compare with each other? I developed tools to analyze the notes collected during the exploration and testing phases to automatically aggregate the information coming from personality assessments at group levels.

Once the model for analyzing the impact of personality assessments on performance was in place, it was ready to be tested. Tests were run at a two-year interval on two companies by interviewing executives, HR professionals, and employees at these companies and collecting information before and after the assessment. The interviews contained a total of 59,291 words that were coded and analyzed. The dependent variables of performance included measures of engagement, behavior alignment (employee versus position), as well as other KPIs like sales volume or client retention.

Using this approach, it was possible to track how managers made inferences and used the results of personality assessments in their day-to-day management. The model helped demonstrate the importance of the characteristics we use for assessing people and making important decisions about them.

FINDINGS FROM THE FIELD

The results of the fieldwork showed that personality assessments are typically used in three areas:

1. Hiring, where personality assessment was first historically implemented in organizations through the assessment of personality traits.

2. People management, particularly in team-building activities and during executive coaching, using assessments that are different than the ones used in hiring, with less psychometric qualities (which are typically assessed on their reliability and validity).

3. Organizational development for assessing large groups of people when reengineering an organization, for instance, after a merger.

Three other broad and more abstract areas of use were identified:

4. Self- and social awareness: personality assessments used by individuals to understand how they function and to better situate

themselves, without any particular connection to a job demand, but for comparing with others.

5. Learning about people: personality assessments used during leadership-development courses to learn about one's work style and the styles of others, with the purpose of improving leadership.

6. Communication: the vocabulary created by the assessment is used to communicate about people, create a collective understanding, and make decisions about them.

Although what these techniques tried to assess converged, the techniques used for certain applications were not used for others. For instance, the personality assessments used for hiring were confined to HR departments and generally impractical for use in any other application.

Thanks to the advent of the Internet and new research on core personality dimensions, the development and research on personality assessments has greatly accelerated since the 1990s, including during the time I conducted this field research and when the GRI survey was devised.

The exploration phase of this research not only revealed the benefits of personality assessments for a variety of applications, but also how they were being used and implemented. The measurements from personality assessments were usually quick to obtain, nuanced, and accurate. The assessments complied with the most stringent norms in psychometrics. Yet, who used the results and how they were understood and applied substantially affected their benefits. The personality assessment techniques I studied differed greatly not just in how they were built, but, moreover, in how they functioned. Some took one hour or more to complete; others were as quick as ten minutes or less. What each assessment measured and the hypothesis it supported differed greatly.

All of the techniques focused on assessing the behavioral characteristics of individuals and veered away from other characteristics like intelligence and competencies. However, some assessments showed personality as a changing variable, something that adapts over time, while others suggested that the dimensions they measured were fixed.

The linguistic aspects of assessment techniques emerged as the most challenging to teach potential users to deploy and use properly. Words convey different meanings for different people; however, traits are assessed and labeled as if the meaning is the same for everyone. A typical example of this is how leadership, which can be expressed and assessed in different ways, has one label.

Every new assessment technique challenges previous ones, including the most basic, natural, and non-verbalized assessment based on our intuition. They compete with each other. It typically takes years for an assessment to reveal its limitations and true identity; thus, the competition between assessments may take years to play out.

Users of the information were clearly not limited to HR experts. They included all individual contributors in search of indicators that would help them grow, develop competences, overcome some weaknesses, and perform better. This naturally included those in charge of human resources, whether recruiters or other HR professionals such as executive coaches and leadership development experts.

The research demonstrated the benefits of executives making use of assessment results to develop the leadership, recruitment, and management of their team and company. At the CEO and executive levels, assessments were used to ease their communication and decisions about people. They greatly facilitated dialogue between the operations and HR.

BEYOND FIELDWORK: THE BIRTH OF THE GRI

Based on my fieldwork, it became clear that personality assessment has an infinite potential for changing how people look and think about each other and build trusted relationships faster—using it properly can dramatically increase the performance of individuals and their organization.

Building on these findings, we devised an assessment that could capture the emotional labor that occurs when individuals act out roles in organizations that are too distant from their natural behavior.

The behaviors to be measured would need to be work-related, based on job requirements, and informed by the various ways of performing and developing leadership. Organizations behave in different ways too. Their behaviors can be synced with those of their teams, positions, and employees.

Building the scales of a personality assessment and checking the validity and reliability of its measurement is a time-consuming process. But by using the Internet to collect measurements, we were able to accelerate the process of sampling and applying the statistics needed to create the scales.

Through testing, we demonstrated that the GRI survey was reliable and valid according to psychometric standards and that it complied with the directives of the Equal Employment Opportunity

Commission (EEOC). The assessment did not result in an adverse impact on people of different sexes, ethnic backgrounds, or ages. In other words, the GRI profile cannot tell a person's age, sex, or cultural origin. We continued performing statistical studies to ensure that the measures were sound for hiring applications.

Once the GRI survey was created and validated, we put into place people analytics and other tools that would assist in its implementation at individual, position, team, and organizational levels. We devised the first learning courses and published the training manuals for executives and HR professionals. The translation and validation of the survey into other languages began as well. New explorations into personality and people management could now begin through the use of this newly created personality assessment tool.

While we do not disclose the "secret sauce" that makes up the GRI's algorithms, we remain deeply interested in how the GRI deploys with users and at client organizations and stay involved to ensure that it does so with efficiency and integrity. Our facilitation and support throughout the training and deployment process has become an important part of the knowledge that comes with the assessment and makes it work.

The GRI has been implemented in companies with users at all levels and along the full range of applications—the six that were observed in our field research. We have also measured and tracked the impact of using the GRI on recruitment, management, and engagement levels of employees and how organizations perform as a whole over time. That information is aggregated and shared with executives so that they can continue to optimize their own performance and that of their organization with the GRI.

ACKNOWLEDGMENTS

Like the GRI itself, this book would never have been possible without the contributions and support of numerous people. Many thanks go to:

Katie Salisbury, the chief editor, for her insights and patience in making the content, which was at times a bit technical, more approachable, clear, and concise, and for providing an overall structure and flow appropriate for our topic. Nicole Phelon for the many iterative discussions that have taken much editing work and many manuscripts into a document that started to make sense for a larger audience. Many thanks to Jeanne Parent who, in the process of finalizing the book, has been so generous with her time, gathering information, interviewing clients, and providing sound advice. Special thanks also to Ellen Belli who was instrumental in putting many pieces of the GRI together with the right language to clearly convey our message. Feedback, guidance, and advice from Karla Olson and review from Jennifer Silva Redmond were decisive in the final moments before we took the book to print.

My cofounder and partner in crime, Jeremy de France, with whom this adventure started in a Palo Alto garage—the way all Silicon

Valley start-ups seem to launch—with the first mock-up in Excel and the first lines of codes for the analytics. Since then, the GRI platform has developed into a mature product, during a time when the Internet itself was undergoing constant micro-revolutions. Jeremy mastered all of it, while keeping the architecture solid as a rock, and providing an increasingly compelling and friendly experience for users.

The consulting associates and partners who were part of the journey early on and made the GRI a highly rewarding experience, at senior levels as well, including Mihai Moghior, Gérard Arnaud, Jorge Albert, Alison Bluestone, Marco Bomprezzi, Antonieta Cinquini, Marcus Clarke, Christine Crandell, Frederic Dyèvre, Susan Finch, Peter Frykman, Lourdes Magalhäes, Tal Moore, Morgan Sanchez, Jose Tolovi, Audrey Tremblay, Brantley Rideau, Geoff Roach, Lisa Wilcox, Dana Johnson, Zacharia El Harouchi, Rachel Kjach, Patricia Dragovic and those of the first hours: Vladimir Gostrer, Rick Schaeffer, and Patty Wilson. All of their input, questions, discussion, feedback, and practical experience in so many different topics have helped the GRI grow. The GRI could not possibly be what it is today without their involvement and commitment.

Our advisory board, from whom I am blessed to have received continuous input and to discuss strategic progress with the GRI: Mark Brewer, Adrian Hall, Nicolas Mercier, George Northup, Gilles Pelisson, Keith Raffel, Karen Rohde, Chris Shipley, and Mark White. Experiencing the GRI and the impact of the seminar from within their respective organizations tremendously helped grow and refine our approach at top levels in companies.

Friends at Vistage International who have provided amazing, provocative discussions along the way. That includes Richard Bell, our chair—who is an insatiable resource for understanding what goes on in people's minds—as well as that of others I had the chance to interact with at Vistage, including Robert Hum, John Apgar, René Lacerte, Helen Dietz, Shawn Rao, Yoshihaki Takahashi, Robert Fils, Hannah Kain, Grant Pierce, Sam Klepper, Mark Seramin, Nick Palmer, Chris Somers, Peter Novak, Andrew Wollenberg, Mark Figueiredo, Jared Mathews, Emily Hall, Rusmin Kudinar, Warren Savage, Jeff Lewis, Alice Hill, Robert Koenigsberg, Alan Sataloff, Carl Schlachte, and Arlene Noodleman. They contributed early with high-value feedback about the platform, the seminar, and also the first drafts of the book.

Colleagues at PI® with whom I made part of the journey in the recruitment and leadership development fields prior to starting the GRI: Robin Wood, Larry Good, Robert Ferrara, François Griveau, Marc Aubé-Choussaud, Joseph Machiah, Yves Djorno, Rudolph and Edith Affentranger, Friedemann Stracke, Fiona Brookwell, and Tommy Kennedy-Bartchukoff.

Those who were involved in my doctoral thesis and influential in challenging established ideas in academia, including Frédéric Wacheux, Jean Gustave Padioleau, Alexandre Dorna, Yann Caillère, Jacques Igalens, as well as Lewis Golberg, Gerard Saucier, and James March. Every single discussion remains a memorable time that inspired what later became the GRI to be taken to a new level.

My wife, Susan, for her review of the first drafts, discussions, numerous inputs and advice, and to my daughters Caroline, Colette, Geneviève, and Melanie for their support. I am blessed to have you in my life and part of GRI's journey, too.

SELECTED BIBLIOGRAPHY

This list of references captures a small fraction of the topics covered in this book. Instead, we chose to simply record the books and articles that have particularly inspired our research and work with the GRI.

Akerlof, George A., and Robert J. Shiller. *Animal Spirits: How Human Psychology Drives the Economy, and Why It Matters for Global Capitalism*. Princeton, NJ: Princeton University Press, 2009.

Allport, Floyd H., and Gordon W. Allport. "Personality Traits: Their Classification and Measurement." *The Journal of Abnormal Psychology and Social Psychology* 16 (1921): 7–40.

Anderson, Philip. "Complexity Theory and Organization Science." *Organization Science* 10, no. 3 (1999): 216–232.

Argyris, Chris. *Personality and Organization: The Conflict Between System and the Individual*. New York: Harper & Row, 1957.

Azevedo, Jane. *Mapping Reality: An Evolutionary Realist Methodology for the Natural and Social Sciences*. Albany, NY: SUNY Press, 1997.

Bandura, Albert. *Social Foundations of Thought and Action: A social Cognitive Theory*. Englewood Cliffs, NJ: Prentice Hall, 1986.

Barrick, Murray R., Michael K. Mount, and Timothy A. Judge. "Personality and Performance at the Beginning of the New Millennium: What Do We Know and Where Do We Go Next?" *Personality and Performance* 9 (2001): 9–30.

Bass, Bernard M. *Bass and Stogdill's Handbook of Leadership: Theory, Research, and Managerial Application.* New York: Free Press, 1990.

Bennis, Warren G. *Organization Development: Its Nature, Origins, and Prospects.* Reading, MA: Addison-Wesley, 1979.

Blumer, Herbert. *Symbolic Interactionism: Perspective and Method.* Englewood Cliffs, NJ: Prentice Hall, 1969.

Cameron, Kim S., Robert E. Quinn, Jeff DeGraff, and Anjan V. Thakor. *Competing Values Leadership: Creating Value in Organizations.* Northampton, MA: Edward Elgar Publishing, 2006.

Clarke, Walter V. "The Construction of an Industrial Selection Personality Test." *The Journal of Psychology* 41 (1956): 379–394.

Collins, Jim C. *Good to Great: Why Some Companies Make the Leap...and Others Don't.* New York: HarperCollins, 2001.

Csikszentmihalyi, Mihaly. *Flow: The Psychology of Optimal Experience.* New York: Harper Perennial Modern Classics, 1990.

Cronbach, Lee J., and Goldine C. Gleser. *Psychological Tests and Personnel Decisions* (2nd ed.). Champaign: University of Illinois Press, 1965.

Deci, Edward L., and Richard M. Ryan. "Motivation, Personality, and Development within Embedded Social Contexts: An Overview of Self-Determination Theory." In *The Oxford Handbook of Human Motivation*, edited by R. M. Ryan, 85–107. Oxford, UK: Oxford University Press, 2001.

Digman, J. M. "Higher-Order Factors of the Big Five." *Journal of Personality and Social Psychology* 71, no. 6 (1997): 1246–1256.

Drucker, Peter. *The Practice of Management.* New York: Harper & Row, 1954.

Eco, Umberto. *The Search for the Perfect Language.* Oxford, UK: Blackwell, 1995.

Eisenhardt, Kathleen M. "Building Theories from Case Study Research." *Academy of Management Review* 14, no. 4 (1989): 532–550.

Eysenck, H. J. *The Structure of Human Personality.* London: Methuen, 1960.

Funder, David C. *The Personality Puzzle* (2nd ed.). New York: Norton, 2001.

Goffman, Erving. *The Presentation of Self in Everyday Life.* New York: Doubleday, 1959.

Goldberg Lewis R. "From Ace to Zombie: Some Explorations in the Language of Personality." In *Advances in Personality Assessment*, edited by C. D. Spielberger and J. N. Butcher, 203–134. Hillsdale, NJ: Lawrence Erlbaum, 1982.

Goldberg Lewis R. "What the Hell Took So Long? Donald W. Fiske and the Big-Five Factor Structure." In *Personality Research, Methods, and Theory: A Festschrift Honoring Donald W. Fiske*, edited by P. E. Shrout and S. T. Fiske. Hillsdale, NJ: Lawrence Erlbaum, 1995.

Goleman, Daniel. *Social Intelligence: The New Science of Human Relationship.* New York: Bantam Books, 2006.

Gough, H. G., and A. B. Heilbrun, Jr. *The Adjective Check List Manual.* Palo Alto, CA: Consulting Psychologists Press, 1983.

Habermas, Jürgen. *The Liberating Power of Symbols: Philosophical Essays.* Cambridge, MA: The MIT Press, 2001.

Hamel, Gary, and C.K. Prahalad. *Competing for the Future: Breakthrough Strategies for Seizing Control of Your Industry and Creating the Markets of Tomorrow.* Boston, MA: Harvard Business School Press, 1994.

Hersey, Paul, Kenneth H. Blanchard, and Dewey E. Johnson. *Management of Organizational Behavior.* Prentice Hall, 1996.

Magnusson, David. (2001). "The Holistic-interactionistic Paradigm: Some Directions for Empirical Developmental Research." *European Psychologist* 6, no. 3 (2001): 153–162.

Herzberg, Frederick. *Work and the Nature of Man.* New York: The World Publishing Company, 1971.

Hogan, J., and R. Hogan. "Theoretical Frameworks for Assessment." In *Individual Psychological Assessment,* edited by R. Jeanneret and R. Sizer. San Francisco: Jossey-Bass (1998).

Judge, Timothy A., Joyce E. Bono, and Edwin A. Locke. "Personality and Job Satisfaction: The Mediating Role of Job Characteristics." *Journal of Applied Psychology* 85 (2000): 237–249.

Jung, C. G. "Psychological Types." *Classics in the History of Psychology.* (1921).

Kahneman, Daniel. *Thinking, Fast and Slow.* New York: Farrar, Strauss and Giroux, 2011.

Kaplan, Robert S., and David P. Norton. "Transforming the Balanced Scorecard from Performance Measurement to Strategic Management Part I." *Accounting Horizons* 15, no. 1 (2001): 87–104.

Keirsey, David. *Please Understand Me II: Temperament, Character, Intelligence.* Del Mar, CA: Prometheus Nemesis Book Company, 1998.

Kelly, George A. *A Theory of Personality: The Psychology of Personal Constructs.* New York: W.W. Norton & Company, 1963.

Korzybski, Alfred. *Science and Sanity.* Brooklyn, NY: Institute of General Semantics, 1933.

Kets de Vries, Manfred F. R., and D. Miller. *The Neurotic Organization: Diagnosing and Changing Counterproductive Styles of Management.* San Francisco: Jossey-Bass, 1984.

Lakatos, Imre, and Alan Musgrave. *Criticism and the Growth of Knowledge.* Cambridge, UK: Cambridge University Press, 1970.

Lievens, F., F. De Fruyt, and K. Van Dam. "Assessors' Use of Personality Traits in Descriptions of Assessment Centre Candidates: A Five-factor Model Perspective." *Journal of Occupational and Organizational Psychology* 74, no. 5 (2001): 623–636.

Linton, Ralph. *The Cultural Background of Personality*. New York: Appleton-Century-Crofts, Inc., 1945.

Magnusson, David. "Holistic Interactionism: A Perspective for Research on Personality Development." In *Handbook of Personality: Theory and Research*, edited by L. A. Pervin and O. P. John, 219–247. New York: Guilford, 1999.

March, James G., and Robert I. Sutton. "Organizational Performance as a Dependant Variable." *Organization Science* 8, no. 6 (1997): 698–706.

Marston, William M. *Emotions of Normal People*. New York: Harcourt, Brace and Company 1928.

Martin, B. A., C. C. Bowen, and S. T. Hunt. "How Effective Are People at Faking on Personality Questionnaires?" *Personality and Individual Differences* 32 (2002): 247–256.

Maslow, Abraham H. "A Theory of Human Motivation." *Psychological Review* 50, (1943): 370–396.

McCormick, E. J. "Job and Task Analysis." In *Handbook of Industrial and Organisational Psychology*, edited by M. D. Dunnette, 651–696. New York: Wiley, 1983.

McCrae, Robert R., and Paul T. Costa. *Personality in Adulthood: A Five-Factor Theory Perspective*. New York: Guilford, 2003.

McGregor, Douglas. *The Human Side of Enterprise*. New York: McGraw-Hill, 1960.

McKelvey, Bill. "Postmodernism vs. Truth in Management Theory." In *Post Modernism & Management: Pros and Cons and Alternatives*, edited by Ed Locke. Amsterdam: Elsevier, 2002.

Mead, George H. "The Social Self." *Journal of Philosophy, Psychology, and Scientific Methods* 10, (1913): 374–380.

Miles M. B., and A. M. Huberman. *Qualitative Data Analysis: An Expanded Sourcebook*. Thousand Oaks, CA: Sage, 1994.

Mischel, Walter. *Personality and Assessment*. Hillsdale, NJ: Lawrence Erlbaum, 1996.

Morgeson Frederick P., and Michael A. Campion. "Social and Cognitive Sources of Potential Inaccuracy in Job Analysis." *Journal of Applied Psychology* 82, no. 5 (1997): 627–655.

Murphy, Kevin R., and Jeanette N. Cleveland. *Performance Appraisal: An Organizational Perspective*. Needham Heights, MA: Allyn & Bacon, 1991.

Parsons, Talcott, and Edward A. Shils. *Toward a General Theory of Action: Theoretical Foundations for the Social Sciences*. New York: Free Press, 2001.

Peirce, Charles S. *Philosophical Writings of Peirce: Selection of Papers Between 1931 and 1935*, edited by J. S. Buchler. New York: Dover Publications, 1935.

Pfeffer, Jeffrey. *Leadership BS: Fixing Workplaces and Careers One Truth at a Time*. New York: HarperCollins Publishers, 2015.

Perrow, Charles. *Complex Organizations: A Critical Essay*. Glenview, IL: Scott Foresman, 1972.

Pervin Lawrence A., and Oliver P. John. *Handbook of Personality: Theory and Research*. New York: Guilford, 1990.

Quine, W. V. *Pursuit of Truth*. Cambridge, MA: Harvard University Press, 1992.

Quinn, Robert E., Regina M. O'Neill, and Lynda St. Clair. *Pressing Problems in Modern Organizations (That Keep Us Up at Night):*

Transforming Agendas for Research and Practice. New York: AMA Publications, 2000.

Rogers, Carl R. "Some Observations on the Organization of Personality." *American Psychologist* 2 (1947): 358–368.

Rogers, Carl R. *On Becoming a Person.* Boston, MA: Houghton Mifflin Company, 1961.

Rorty, Richard. *Philosophy and Social Hope.* London, England: Penguin Books, 1999.

Saucier, Gerard. "Mini-Markers: A Brief Version of Goldberg's Unipolar Big-Five Markers." *Journal of Personality Assessment* 63, no. 3 (1994): 506–516.

Saucier, Gerard, and Lewis R. Goldberg. "The Structure of Personality Attributes." In *Personality and Work*, edited by M. R. Barrick and A. M. Ryan, 1–29. San Francisco: Jossey-Bass, 2002.

Schaeffer, Nora C., and Stanley Presser. "The Science of Asking Questions." *Annual Review of Sociology* 29 (2003): 65–88.

Schmit, Mark J., Jenifer A. Kihm, and Chet Robie. "Development of a Global Measure of Personality." *Personnel Psychology* 53, no. 1 (2000): 153–193.

Schwartz, Shalom H. "Are There Universal Aspects in the Structure and Contents of Human Values?" *Journal of Social Issues* 50, no. 4 (1994).

Seelig, Tina. *Insight Out: Get Ideas Out of Your Head and Into the World.* New York: HarperCollins Publishers, 2015.

Shaw, Patrick. *Logic and Its Limits.* New York: Oxford University Press, 1997.

Simons, R. "The Role of Management Control Systems in Creating Competitive Advantage: New Perspectives." *Accounting, Organizations, and Society* 15, no. 1/2 (1990): 127–143.

Sternberg, Robert J. "The Concept of Intelligence and Its Role in Lifelong Learning and Success." *Amerian Psychologist* 52, no. 10 (1997): 1030–1037.

Thurstone, Louis L. *The Measurement of Values*. Chicago: The University of Chicago Press, 1959.

Vroom, Victor H. *Work and Motivation*. New York: Wiley, 1964.

Weick, Karl E. *The Social Psychology of Organizing*. San Francisco, CA: McGraw-Hill, 1979.

Wiggins, Jerry S., et al. *The Five-Factor Model of Personality: Theoretical Perspectives*. NY: The Guilford Press. 1996.

CPSIA information can be obtained
at www.ICGtesting.com
Printed in the USA
FSHW012314081218
54303FS